Beauty and Light:
Mystical Discourses of
A Contemporary Female Sufi Master

T0307199

Beauty and Light: Mystical Discourses of A Contemporary Female Sufi Master

by Cemalnur Sargut

Edited by Tehseen Thaver

Translator: Cangüzel Zülfikar
Assistant Translators: Ömer Çolakoğlu
and Nazlı Kayahan

FONS VITAE

First published in 2017 by
Fons Vitae
49 Mockingbird Valley Drive
Louisville, KY 40207
http://www.fonsvitae.com
Email: fonsvitaeky@aol.com

Library of Congress Control Number: 2017956383

ISBN 978-1-941610-06-0

Original Turkish language edition published by Nefes Press
Copyright 2012 by Cemalnur Sargut

English language edition published by Fons Vitae
Copyright 2017; translated by Cangüzel Zülfikar

Printed in Canada

The most profound gratitude goes to Anne Ogden, without
whose editing, proofreading, and tireless service this important volume would not have come to be. Great appreciation
is extended to Emma Proietti for her careful editing.

Cover photograph by Mehmet Okutan

Contents

Foreword

I cannot remember the first time I met Cemalnur Sargut.

I have tried and tried to remember, but it is truly as if I have always known her. Perhaps that is as it should be, to have met in that place beyond places (*la makan*) and in that time before there was such a thing as time (*la zaman*).

One of the first memories I have from sitting with Cemalnur is from a magical night in Istanbul, where we were treated to a night of her *Sohbet*, mystical discourse. Hour after hour went by, and Cemalnur was sharing stories, anecdotes, Sufi aphorism, commentary on the Qur'an, and more. It all seemed so.... effortless. These were not her stories. They were *pouring* through her. It was as if she had simply emptied herself of her own ego, and she was a channel of grace to the magical Beyond.

I remember turning to a friend who was there, Professor Carl Ernst, a leading scholar of Sufism, and one of us said to the other: "She is one of those people that you and I have read about in books our whole lives."

Another time when she came to North Carolina, we sat in the living room of my dear friends Cangüzel, Fahir, and Yekta. I remember coming in for a "short visit." I stayed for almost eight hours in that room. She sat there with no notes, no books, no lesson plans, but this *Sohbet* poured out of her. Story after story, anecdote after anecdote. And the amazing part is that in the context of her mystical discourses, time and again she touched on so many issues that I was struggling with and going through. I remember looking around at one point at the other friends in the room, wondering what they were doing there. Clearly, this was all so tailormade for me! (It's a common experience of novices, with the ego still perceiving the world through our own needs and desires). I remember Cangüzel and Fahir serving tea and a beautiful simple meal, people getting up for bathroom breaks and prayers, but we stayed together. She wove together story after story, dropping gem after gem. No one left, no one was tired. I could have stayed for eight more hours, and eight beyond that, and eight more eternities beyond all of them.

Over the last fifteen years, I have had the blessing of visiting Cemalnur and her circle of friends again and again. There's something about experiencing a *Sohbet* with her that is a reminder of how thin the veils between this world and the next world can become. I remember when she published a book on the first ten verses of the second chapter of the Qur'an that was hundreds of pages long. Even for those of us who have spent years of our lives studying great masterpieces like Rumi's *Mathnawi*, she dives into the ocean of these texts with such effortless grace, making connections that mere scholars had never seen before. I realized that mere academic scholarship floats on the surface of the ocean, whereas she swims deep, deep inside.

And the sheer outpouring of insight is something mindboggling. I remember reading about prodigious scholars, like Ibn 'Arabi having around 800 works attributed to them. One of them alone, *Futuhat al-Makiyya*, is published in numerous volumes that take up a whole shelf. Rumi wrote tens of thousands of lines of poetry, with one of them, the *Divan-e Shams,* filling a whole row on my bookshelf. This achievement has seemed incredible to many scholars, who have ended up debating and disputing the productivity of any human. Sitting at the feet of Cemalnur, that level of productivity does not seem so inconceivable. Where does this inspiration come from?

The word *Sohbet*, which is sometimes translated as "mystical discourse" actually comes from the Arabic root word *Suhba*, which is Fellowship. To sit in the presence of these friends of God (Arabic: *awliya*, Turkish: *evliya*) is to have a taste of what it would be like to share in the fellowship of and with the Prophets. The sweetness of *Sohbet* and insha'Llah, the sweetness of reading this volume, is but a taste of what it must be like to sit with the ones who make God real, Here and Now.

Before moving on to the *Sohbet* stories of Cemalnur, so beautifully edited and curated by Professor Tehseen Thaver, let me make three points about how these stories are listened to in a Sufi context.

The "meaning" of *Sohbet* is always generated through a context of a relationship. In other words, a story does not simply "mean" something by itself. The meanings are often specific to the individual devotee, and different meanings might be intended for different listeners.

In the years of listening to Cemalnur's *Sohbets*, I have had the privilege of hearing some of the same teaching stories again and again. They have become familiar friends: the story of the dwarf cousin who was so grateful to God that she wouldn't give up her short stature, or the Rumi tale of the Greeks and the Chinese painters. There is the temptation to treat these old guests as "I have heard this before," but the "you" who is hearing them now is the not the same as the previous "you." So there is a new meaning in each re-telling. And part of the magic and blessing of the *Sohbet* is for the listener to prepare herself/himself each time to remain open, attentive, vigilant, and receive the stories.

Lastly, there is the question of how these stories actually are the very lessons of the Sufi path. It is not merely that they *contain* Sufi wisdom. No, the *Sohbet* itself is Sufi wisdom. Everything about being in the presence of the teacher, being present with an open and receptive heart, the stories that come at one like waves from the ocean, the whole notion of living in an enchanted universe, being open and receptive towards the Divine, and the personalizing of wisdom in a communal setting...this is the Sufi path.

Through the words of Cemalnur, there are a few themes that come up again and again. It is good to welcome them as we move through these *Sohbets*.

Tawhid (Tevhid). For most Muslims it refers to the oneness of God. Sufis like Cemalnur already know that God is one. Unity for them is more, so much more. So *Tawhid* also refers to the need for each of us to become one, to become whole, inside our own self. And we as a human community have to become united, we have to become one, before we can become reflections of the One.

Radical Love (Eshq). Cemalnur's Sufi teachings come from the path of Radical Love tradition that has been expressed through the centuries through the teachings of the Prophet Muhammad, Abu 'l-Hasan Kharaqani, Mawlana Rumi, and others. And it is this love (*Eshq* in Persian, *Aşk* in Turkish) that is the supreme path to God.

*Need for a spiritual mentor. One would not pick up a book on "Complete Idiots Guide to Brain Surgery" and proceed to perform brain surgery on a patient. One would be expected to shadow physicians, and learn by walking in their footsteps. Sufis are like this, they see themselves as being experts of the heart, masters of the realm of the spirit. And one would not be expected to learn merely by reading Sufi books, but rather by following in the footsteps of a mystical guide. Cemalnur's teachings place a great deal of emphasis on the need for a *Murshid*, a spiritual guide.

Insan-e Kamil (Complete Human Being). Part of the *Sohbet* tradition focuses on the fact that we have to become a complete human being, a mature human being. Using metaphors from Rumi, Cemalnur emphasizes the need to move from being "raw" to being "cooked" to becoming "on fire." This journey often involves tests and tribulations, and the willingness to welcome pain and suffering.

With these few words, let us friends go and sit down for the waves of beauty and mercy that pour through Cemalnur. You are in for a treat.

Bismillah.

Omid Safi
Professor of Islamic Studies
Duke University

Acknowledgements

First of all I would like to thank Cemalnur *abla* for the invaluable opportunity to engage with and learn from her wisdom and thought. The production of this book went through several stages. Cangüzel Zülfikar, Ömer Çolakoğlu, and Nazlı Kayahan played a critical role in the translation of the Turkish text. In addition, Cangüzel went the extra mile by assisting with problems and queries of all sorts throughout the process of editing and compiling this book. Many thanks also to Gray Henry for her steadfast support throughout the execution of the project; her energy for and investment in this book was crucial at all stages, from its conceptualization to its eventual production. This book would not have reached fruition without the excellent counsel and wisdom extended by Omid Safi. He has been a pillar of support, and also very kindly took out the time to write a wonderful foreword. Many thanks to Belgin Batum for excavating and providing the set of pictures that made possible the photographic essay. Thanks also to Neville Blakemore and Steve Stives for their extraordinary patience and diligence during the production process. Yekta Zülfikar and Najeeba Khan also volunteered their time by extending important editorial help. Support from the Bard research fund allowed me to take out time towards the completion of this project.

Tehseen Thaver
Assistant Professor of Religion
Bard College

Sufi Charismatic Authority in the Contemporary World: Introducing Cemalnur Sargut

Cemalnur Sargut, the Turkish leader of the Rifaʻi Sufi order, occupies a special place in the intellectual and social landscape of contemporary Islam. This is so for multiple reasons. As a female Sufi teacher who commands a loyal and active worldwide following, especially in Turkey, Sargut's career as a scholar and Sufi leader represents an important case study in the dynamics of contemporary global Sufism. This volume represents the first text in English translation that brings together some of her major discourses and teachings as presented to her students through the genre of oral discourses. More specifically, the discourses that form the core of this book were collected through oral interviews with Cemalnur, conducted by her students as part of a weekly program aired on a national Turkish radio station. The original Turkish transcription on which this English translation is based is titled *Dinle* (*Listen*), and was published in 2012 by Nefes press.[1]

Cemalnur has been actively training disciples and students in the teachings and practices of the Rifaʻi Sufi order for the last forty years. While her oral and written discourses are widely available in Turkish, they have until now remained inaccessible to an English language audience. This book seeks to address this lacuna by introducing key aspects of her thought and spiritual orientation in English. In this brief introduction I wish to provide readers a broad outline of the key themes and concepts that animate the lineaments of Cemalnur's thought as presented in this book. In addition, I hope to provide readers with the intellectual and institutional context in which one might be able to place Cemalnur's thought and scholarly career. Moreover, I will have occasion to discuss the literary genre within Sufism and Islamic literature that corresponds to the kind

---

1. *Dinle*, (Istanbul: Nefes press), 2012.

of oral teachings and sermons that populate the pages of this book. Finally I will briefly explain the stylistic decisions and choices that were made in the presentation of this text.

BIOGRAPHY

The most indubitable influence on Sargut's intellectual and spiritual development is Kenan Rifa'i (1867-1950), the revered leader of one branch of the Rifa'i Sufi order. A noted educator, musician and composer, Rifa'i was born in Salonica in current day Greece (the Rifa'i order is named after its founder Ahmed Rifa'i (d. 578/1182) from Iraq). Kenan Rifa'i's spiritual lineage, instruction and authorization is also tied to teachers of three other Sufi orders: the Mevlevi order (founded in the name of Jalal al-Din Rumi (d. 672/1273)), Qadiri order (founded by Abdul Qadir Jilani (d. 561/1166) and Shadhili order (that derived its name from its founder Abu al-Hasan al-Shadhili (d. 656/1258).

Sargut was first introduced to Sufi teachings through her mother, Meşküre Sargut (d. 2013), herself a devoted disciple of Kenan Rifa'i. In addition to her mother, another important influence on Sargut was Samiha Ayverdi (1905-1993), a close disciple of Kenan Rifa'i from a young age. Ayverdi was a prominent Sufi intellectual, a strong proponent of educational reform in Turkey's newly established Republic, and an accomplished novelist whose nostalgic writings on Ottoman history and culture are both a lament of a culture lost as well as a manifesto for its preservation. It was Ayverdi who first instructed Sargut to begin teaching Rumi's *Mathnawi* and later entrusted Sargut to another teacher, Hayri Bilecik, with whom Sargut studied the Qur'an and Rumi's *Mathnawi* more formally.

It is useful to note that although there are many mentions in the present text by Sargut to "my teacher," by whom she means Kenan Rifa'i, Sargut never actually met Rifa'i in person. Yet Sargut speaks about him as a devoted disciple would speak about her spiritual teacher, indicative of an intimate master/disciple relationship and of the magisterial authority he holds in the genealogy of Rifa'i teachers. The temporal distance that lies between Sargut and Rifa'i is of no consequence here, as she relies on a notion of sacral time (as opposed to secular conceptions of time as linear) whereby the everyday sequence of events is interwoven with and mediated by characters, episodes and events of a higher time.

Institutional Terrain

Sargut's own personal, professional and spiritual journey serves as an exemplary devotional model for her students. It is not uncommon to hear her offer anecdotes from her own life as moral teachings for her talks. Sargut completed a degree in chemical engineering and started her career as a high school chemistry teacher. She continued in this role for twenty years, and distinguished herself as a passionate and selfless educator who above all cared deeply for her students. At the age of twenty-four, following Ayverdi's instructions, she began to lead reading groups on Rumi's *Mathnawi*; her audience at that time comprised of medical students and high school students. As time passed, she began to devote more and more time to the teaching of Sufism and the Qur'an, until she retired from her position as a high school teacher and dedicated herself solely to teaching Sufism.

Sargut currently has a markedly globalized and public dimension to her role as spiritual leader of the Rifa'i order. This is to say that while she follows her predecessors in placing a strong emphasis on the interiorized nature of spiritual teachings, she simultaneously navigates distinctly modern technologies in conveying those teachings – technologies that include the media, academia, and the secular terrain of Turkish civil society. Let me elaborate on her role in each of these domains.

Sargut is director of the Istanbul chapter of the Turkish Women's Cultural Association (TÜRKKAD), a non-profit organization dedicated to promoting cultural awareness of Turkish/Islamic arts, preserving traditional crafts such as calligraphy and miniatures, and offering educational opportunities to low-income students. TÜRKKAD was founded in 1966 by Samiha Ayverdi, and can be seen as part of a wider revival of NGOs in Turkey after the proclamation of the Republic in 1923 and the subsequent shutting down of dervish lodges and religious schools as the government tightened its grip over Islamic foundations. It was at this time that numerous groups with religious, charitable, and social agendas sought to reorganize under the banner of NGOs. TÜRKKAD's image as an organization that promotes the cultural arts and heritage of Turkey plays a critical logistical function for Sargut, namely that of enabling her to enter into a markedly regulated public sphere of Turkey's secular terrain.

Under Sargut's leadership, TÜRKKAD and its partner organizations (Kerim Education, Culture and Health Foundation and the in-house press, Nefes Academy) have placed a strong emphasis on the teaching of Sufism, humanities, and the social sciences, positioning themselves as centers that seek to advocate these disciplines in a variety of ways. Nefes regularly publishes books on the subject of Sufism, some authored by Sargut, others by other renowned scholars. In addition, these organizations host large-scale academic conferences with Sufi themes, inviting both international and Turkish scholars. Aside from this wide range of public activities within Turkey, Sargut has also worked with these organizations to establish long-term relationships with academic institutions across the world. Namely, they have endowed chaired positions in Islamic Studies at the University of North Carolina at Chapel Hill (2009) and Peking University in Beijing, China (2011). More recently, the Kenan Rifa'i Center for Sufi Studies was established at Kyoto University in Japan (2016), and the Institute for Sufi Studies was established at Üsküdar University in Istanbul, Turkey (2014). Thus Sargut, very much in line with the vision and approach of Rifa'i and Ayverdi before her, approaches academia as a critical medium through which to disseminate Sufi teachings in Turkey's current sociopolitical and religious climate.

In addition to these leadership roles within Sufi and intellectual communities, Sargut is no less than a celebrity figure in contemporary Turkey. She maintains a visible and popular profile in the public domain through regular appearances on television and radio, as well as her biweekly oral lectures on the Qur'an and select Sufi texts. Sargut is also a social welfare and development activist, and a much sought-after public speaker at various national and international venues. Finally, Sargut is an acclaimed author of Sufism with at least twelve publications to date, ranging from commentaries on select verses of the Qur'an to transcribed radio interviews on individual prophets and Sufism more broadly.

STUDENTS

Even on a regular day, it would be difficult to find Sargut without the retinue of disciples that surround her at all times. Her students number in the thousands and are scattered across Turkey and worldwide. Their demographic backgrounds vary widely in all respects – gender, class, nationality, sect, and race – but the majority are highly educated Turkish women with well established careers, including architects, artists, professors, medical doctors, and businesswomen. In fact, her male disciples have jokingly complained about the limited access and time that they get with Sargut due to the fierce competition they face from her female students. In the past, Sargut has sought to redress these concerns by scheduling lectures exclusively for this male constituency.

Sargut's relationship with her students is largely informal and jovial. They gather regularly for the public discourses, and privately for the ritual singing of religious poems (*ilahiyat*) – many composed by Kenan Rifa'i – for the celebration and commemoration of important religious occasions and life's milestones, and for impromptu lecture-sermons that extend into full day affairs at various locations across the city. In addition, a different mix of students meets with Sargut almost daily after dawn for a brisk walk on the boardwalk, followed by breakfast in one of the students' homes - a gathering that quickly moves from relaxed banter to serious oral sermon. The themes for these sermons are often determined by specific questions suggested by the students, animated by challenges from their daily lives. All these gatherings serve to cultivate a strong sense of community, held together by the shared bond of loyalty to Sargut, their spiritual counsel and teacher. The structure of this relationship however, goes beyond the grammar of linear subservience. In fact, it is not uncommon for students to frame the impact of their individual life choices, be they dietary, familial or intellectual, as products of Sargut's impact on them. To a marked extent then, there is an embodied quality to this relationship, where the intimate connection between student and teacher is formulated in the form of what anthropologist Saba Mahmood, in a different context, has aptly called "cohabitation."[2]

PEDAGOGY OF ORAL DISCOURSE

As the spiritual leader and teacher of a Sufi community, Sargut's goal is to play an active role in the ethical-moral formation of her students and other listeners. One of the most important strategies and media that Sargut employs to achieve this larger objective is that of the oral sermon (*sohbet*). Several times during the week, Sargut addresses her students through the lecture-sermon format

2. Saba Mahmood, "Religious Reason and Secular Affect: An Incommensurable Divide?" in *Critical Inquiry*, 35, no. 4 (2009): p. 842.

in the setting of municipal lecture halls that are open to the wider public. It is within this literary genre of the lecture-sermon that the present text, *Beauty and Light,* is situated. This book represents a compilation of the discourses that were broadcast between 2003-2004 on the national Turkish Alevi radio station, Cem Radyo, on which Sargut was featured. The quick pace and accessible narrative style of the live conversation is preserved in this transcribed text through the question and answer format in which it is structured. The conversations are organized around five central topics: Sufism, proper conduct, divine decree/destiny, prayer, and sacrifice/ pilgrimage. The hosts, Nazlı Kayahan and Neşe Taş (Sargut's students) ask Sargut a series of questions concerning these themes, most often pushing Sargut to rephrase, simplify, and further elaborate on the ideas she presents.

While Sargut's lectures were aired on the radio, the literary form of the "lecture-sermons" that she employed possesses a long-running history in the tradition of Sufi pedagogical methods. 'Abd al-Qadir Jilani, the towering founder of the Qadiri Sufi order, was among one of the earliest figures to have adopted the public exhortation style—often termed *maqalat* (utterances)—for disseminating his teachings. Characteristic to the genre is the discussion of various aspects of a seeker's relationship to God, and of the spiritual discipline required to progress in that relationship. Another closely related Sufi literary genre is that of the discourse or conference form, *malfuzat* (literally, "expressions, utterances"). This form has survived in multiple languages, most notably in Persian, and Rumi's *Spiritual Discourses (Fihi Ma Fihi)* represents among the earliest models for works of this type. Within such works it was common for the speaker to cover a wide range of topics, often as disparate issues within a single session.[3] Perhaps what distinguishes Sargut's discourses from those of her Sufi predecessors are the rather distinct locations in which they occur: not traditional Sufi lodges or private homes but talk shows, radio interviews, and public municipal auditoriums. Sargut, quite literally, and quite deliberately, has publicized her teachings.

KNOWLEDGE, AFFECT, NARRATIVE

Sargut draws on multiple sources for her discussion, including

---

3. John Renard, *Seven Doors to Islam: Spirituality and the Religious Life of Muslims,* (Berkeley: University of California Press), 1996, p. 186-190.

verses from the Qur'an, Prophetic sayings, and teachings of various Sufi figures. The two texts that stand out, however, and constantly inform her thought, are Rumi's *Mathnawi* and *Fihi ma Fihi*. Both of these works are the key that connects for Sargut the density of Sufi thought with the ethereality of everyday life. In her own words, "Each narrative is an outward reflection of events that we experience within ourselves." Accordingly, the defining characteristic that shapes Sargut's oral discourses is her employment of storytelling as a major literary device. Narrative serves several important functions for Sargut. First, it enables a wider reach of listeners and enlivens the general content of her talks. Second, and perhaps even more importantly, it effectively encapsulates and communicates the overarching pedagogy that is central to Sargut's style of moral teaching: a pedagogy that brings together wit, wisdom, humor, and the deep compassion and intimacy she shares with her students. This is to say that Sargut's oral discourses do not simply "inform" her listeners about correct moral practice. Rather, they seek to cultivate correct practice by attuning the audience to the acquisition of such moral instruction.

Intervening for her students at the level of the "affective," Sargut's lectures aim to cultivate what I term a living "Qur'anic Sufi community." In her own words, spiritual discourses are there "to increase our love; we need these discourses in order to nourish a person's love. What feeds love are the feelings a person encounters during a spiritual discourse." She continued, rather evocatively, "all our talk and discussion about love thus far has the same objective: to understand the meaning of God, to find that Beloved in ourselves, to unite with that Beloved, to meet with that Beloved, and to take each breath with that Beloved." In another instance, Sargut explains the critical role of the body in this learning encounter: "the body functions as host, capable of embodying the divine attributes, perfected and exemplified by earlier prophets, saints and spiritual teachers." According to this framing, the morally-attuned body enables a specific sensibility and sociability, which Sargut as spiritual teacher seeks to inspire and instill in her students.

Furthermore, Sargut's oral sermons are animated by a desire to invoke awe, wonder, and gratitude rather than simply offering answers to the question of what moral-ethical practice constitutes. In other words, the experience of learning from Sargut does not represent a purely intellectualized exercise of meaning-production whereby knowledge is detached from its agent, audience, and their embodied practices. More crucial to her pedagogy is the affective dimension of learning whereby corporeal proximity and an otological (listening) bond between teacher and student enable both bodily and spiritual transformation.

NOTES ON TRANSLITERATION AND CONVENTIONS

In the presentation of this text, I have adopted the following stylistic, translation, and transliteration procedures. Turkish transliterations follow a modified system that is based on the standard of the *International Journal of Middle East Studies*. Use of diacritical markings is minimized to make the text accessible to an English reader. Some exceptions to this include instances when phonetically suitable Roman equivalents were not available, as in "*Şeriat.*"

Sufi vocabulary based on Arabic and Persian loan words in Turkish is on first appearance translated into the English, with the Turkish spelling in brackets, and where applicable, is followed by transliteration of the Arabic/Persian spelling. For example, "unicity (*Tevhid,* Ar. *Tawhid*)." There are two exceptions to this: first, in the case of proper names and book titles, and second, in the case of Qur'an chapter titles and phrases. In both cases, I have only provided the transliteration with the Arabic spelling.

There are also a few terms that I render in the Turkish without translation while providing a definition when they first appear (for example, *edep*). Finally, the semantic field occupied by some Turkish terms is expansive (such as *hükm, istidat*) such that their meaning is best conveyed through a variety of terms in English. I render those terms into English in a manner that best fits the particular context of discussion. The citations and references found in the footnotes are mine. I have included them as an aid to the reader. They are not part of Cemalnur's oral discourse that occupies the main text.

Throughout the text, the questions are posed by Sargut's students, Nazlı Kayahan and Neşe Taş, (indicated by "Q" and in bold font), followed by her responses (indicated by "A").

In the original Turkish transcript of the radio interviews, Sargut and the program hosts preface the names of revered personalities like Prophet Muhammad and other sacred personalities with epithets such as "sultan" and "*hazret* (presence)." These have been removed for the following reason: the work that these honorifics perform in the Turkish is to ensure and preserve an overall tone of reverence. There is a long tradition attached to this practice, such that their absence in the Turkish would be noticeable. In contemporary English, the addition of honorifics seems rather extraneous and burdensome for the reader.

Finally, with respect to dates, the Islamic lunar calendar (*hijri*) dates are listed first, followed by the Gregorian year, for example, (d. 578/1182).

Tehseen Thaver
Assistant Professor of Religion
Bard College

Chapter One: .
Sufism (*Tasavvuf*)

Q: Can you explain Kenan Rifa'i's understanding of Sufism (*tasavvuf*)?

A: Sufism is a journey to the depths of one's being.

Religion (*din*), in addition to its prescriptions for outward behavior, also entails a process of inner cleansing. This process entails continuous spiritual struggle (*riyazat*), control of the insatiable desires of the soul (*nefis*, Ar. *nafs*), and purification in what we might call a "vessel of spiritual rehabilitation." This process of inner cleansing helps people evolve into spiritually perfected beings, and endows them with an unshakable spiritual integrity.

My teacher, Kenan Rifa'i, has said in his book, *Discourses*, that professing to have beautiful manners does not deliver us from the hell of ignorance and heedlessness of the Truth.[1] Nor does it enable us to be among the intimate friends who inhabit the true paradise of pre-eternal nearness. Intimate friends are those who have realized the primordial condition granted to each human being at the time of creation. It is also not helpful to simply say, "I have no needs." Instead one must actively cleanse oneself of the spiritual impurities that have accumulated from the love of this world, cast off ignorance and heedlessness from one's soul, and allow the spirit (*ruh*) – its essential qualities and inherent purity – to triumph.

---

1. Kenan Rifa'i, *Sohbetler*, (Istanbul: Kubbealti Neşriyati, 3rd edition, 2009), p. 474.

It is Sufism, or the mystical core and essence of Islam, that directs us on this path of purification. Sufism illuminates the path for those who aspire towards this goal.

Sufism is the awareness of God's ever-watchful presence at the time of our every undertaking. It is to be mindful of this with every breath. It is to bear the weight of responsibility in every action, and to strive to treat others as if it is none other than God we are interacting with. The path of Sufism is thus a set of special practices laid out for the seeker to follow conscientiously, seriously, sincerely, and entirely. According to Abdul Qadir al-Jilani (d. 561/1166),[2] every letter in the term "*tasavvuf* (Ar. *tasawwuf)*" carries a distinct meaning[3]:

"T" for *tevbe* (Ar. *tawba*) (repentance)
"S" for *safa* (purification)
"V" for *velayet* (Ar. *wilaya*) (intimacy, friendship (with God))
"F" for *fena* (Ar. *fana*) (annihilation)

Sufism is built on eight pillars. The first pillar is generosity, the attribute of the Prophet Abraham (Ibrahim). The second is contentment, the attribute of the Prophet Isaac (Ishaq). The third is patience, the attribute of the Prophet Job (Ayyub). The fourth is discernment, that is, realizing the hand of God in every event, and it is the attribute of the Prophet Zachariah (Zakariyya). The fifth is intimacy, the attribute of the Prophet John (Yahya). The sixth is Sufism, or the inner quest for meaning, and it is the attribute of the Prophet Moses (Musa). The seventh is Love, the attribute of the Prophet Jesus (Isa). The eighth is complete poverty, or the total realization of one's status as servant, and this is the station of our beloved master, the Prophet Muhammad Mustafa, may the peace and blessings of God be upon him.

Whoever understands the truth and secret of a collective mystical audition session (*sema*) and remembrance session (*zikr*), for them, the material body becomes the Sufi lodge (*tekke*) and the heart their real abode.

---

2. Twelfth century Persian Sufi and Hanbali jurist based in Baghdad, founder of the Qadiriyya Sufi order.

3. The letters that form the word tasawwuf are "t," "s," "w," and "f." In the Arabic script, short vowels are indicated by vowel diacritics (*harakat*), not by letters.

According to Junayd Baghdadi (d. 298/910),[4] Sufism is God's taking of the soul of His servant and replacing it with a new form of life with and in Himself. Sufism is not established in a person's life by paying lip service to its essential tenets, nor through ostentatious discourse; it is achieved by renouncing the hunger for material addictions, habits, desires, and all that is dear to the soul.

One day, when asked what Sufism is, Kenan Rifa'i replied: "Knowledge of the enlightened heart (*gönül*)." He explained:

> There is not a single thing, simple or complex, that is not designed by God's will. It is your spirit and intellect that govern your being. The spirit of the spirit is God. It is His meaning that makes things move and come to a rest. The meaning of the meaning is God again. Thus, it is fitting for a person to leave the spirit to the spirit, thereby making it possible for the spirit to see itself with its own eye. All material beings have come into being in order to point to particular realities and meanings. The human being is the meaning of the universe. It is for this reason that Mevlana Rumi (d. 672/1273)[5] says, "Ever since the House of God (Ka'ba) was built, God has not dwelt in it; yet there is nothing in the house of my heart except Him." Sufism is the quest to acquire this knowledge. However, as Plato also stressed, this knowledge cannot be learnt from books. A human being can unearth it in the treasure of his heart through the process of unceasing contemplation, which kindles the sacred fire of his essential source.

Let's discuss this further. Sufism is not limited to what the religion prescribes for us, such as offering the five daily prayers, fasting, observing supererogatory worship for most of the night, or immersing oneself in charitable actions. It must be understood that God manifests Himself through human beings, together with His actions, words, attributes, and essence, as well as His complete inner and outer control in managing the affairs of the universe.

---

4. Junayd Baghdadi was a famous mystic from amongst the early generation of (recorded) Sufi figures.

5. Mevlana Jalal al-Din Rumi, the thirteenth century theologian, jurist, mystic, and most widely read Sufi poet. In Turkey, Rumi is also referred to simply as "*Mevlana*" or "our master," attesting to the privileged place he holds as poet, mystic and teacher.

Therefore, God's mercy, bounties, severity, wrath, in short, all His attributes are made manifest to human beings through human beings. When we consider this, and recognize that each thing exists and each event comes to pass only with the permission of God, whom then, can you hurt? And by whom can you possibly get hurt? Our worldly bodies are nothing but agents for God's words and actions. God's actions are to be found in apparent and hidden things. However, human beings continue to attribute the power behind all these actions to themselves. Whereas this limited power and control over the management of one's affairs is a loan and a trust. This is the meaning of the saying of the Messenger of God, "He who knows himself knows his Lord."

Q: How is it possible to see the unicity of God in multiplicity?

"The multiplicity of creation in the cosmos does not block our perception of God's oneness, just as the waves do not interfere with the oneness of the sea. Consider our habit of counting, 'one, two, and three...' But is there such a thing as 'two' in reality? Two is the repetition of one. We understand that the existence of all numbers is but the repetition of one. In other words, no number exists except one. It is always the oneness of being (*vahdet-i vücut*; Ar. *wahdat al-wujud*). When you attain knowledge of unicity, you start seeing both the 'doer' and the 'object' as God alone. This is why Abu Bakr said, 'I have not seen anything in which I did not see God.' Once you fully grasp this, you can't look down on anything, be it a cat, a dog, an onion, or a piece of garlic."[6]

For Kenan Rifa'i, the entire universe is the manifestation of God in this world. Accordingly, he says, "There is light in every particle; there is a predetermined manifestation in every drop of water." In this way, he regards the entire cosmos as the locus of God's self-disclosure. For Kenan Rifa'i, all interactions with the things of this world are encounters with God.

He exalts and praises the things of this world, well aware that these are direct manifestations of God. Most importantly, he loves

---

6. Cited in Samiha Ayverdi, Safiye Erol, Nezihe Araz, Sofi Huri, *Ken'an Rifa'i ve Yirminci Asrın Işığında Müslümanlık (Kenan Rifa'i: Being Muslim in the 20th century)*, (Istanbul: Kubbealtı Neşriyatı, 1951), p. 223.

the things of this world. Loves! In my opinion, what is of utmost importance here is that Kenan Rifa'i rescued "love of God" from being reduced to an abstract concept and brought it into the concrete realm of this world and into creation. This is to say he transformed a potentiality into a de facto lifestyle, and changed intention to action.

Shams Tabrizi (d. 645/1247)[7] conveys the same idea when he remarks, "Words are for deeds, deeds are not for words."

This shows that Sufism is not a form of knowledge but a way of life; a path taught to seekers by Perfected Humans (al-*insan al-kamil*).

Kenan Rifa'i notes, "Sufism is eternal, it is to observe the proper etiquette (*edep*; Ar. *adab*)[8] in every situation and at all times."

Sufism is beautiful conduct (*güzel ahlak*; Ar. *akhlaq*); it is to endow oneself with *edep* internally and externally. Inner *edep* is the ability to see God with awe and admiration in everything and everywhere. As Kenan Rifa'i said, Sufism is the ability to see the Real Doer in every action. Outer *edep* is to treat every person and every thing with moderation, equity, veneration, and loving tolerance, all of which stem from inner *edep*.

"Sufism is nothing in speech, but it is everything in the heart. Sufism is the knowledge of the heart."[9]

Sufism is the adoption of correct attitudes, so that the meaning of "There is no god but God" can manifest. It is the ability to see this manifestation in fire, light, abundance, and poverty, in the unbeliever and the believer. It is to know that we are not separate from God, so we should not seek Him outside of ourselves. The veil between God and us is our body.

Sufism is to contemplate the Whole (*kül*); to behold God and His reflection in the human soul. "To behold" is a human predisposition – it is enabled when the seeker of Truth is subjected to a discipline perfectly in line with Sufism; where and when need be, they are able to make any kind of sacrifice, relinquish their rights,

---

7. The thirteenth century saint/friend of God, whose disciple was Jalal al-Din Rumi. Their first encounter in Konya marked the most important turning point in Rumi's life.

8. The term "*edep*" in the context of Sufism evokes the meaning of moral etiquette or "proper respect and courtesy, or principles of conduct regarding God in every aspect of one's spiritual life, whose expression, Ibn 'Arabi indicates, varies greatly according to one's inner state or rank." See James Morris, *Ibn 'Arabi: The Meccan Revelations* (co-author with W. Chittick), New York, Pir Press, 2002, p. 270.

9. Ayverdi, *Kenan Rifa'i*, p. 222.

and endure different kinds of deprivation, affliction, and loss.

Q: What do Sufis say about heaven and hell?

A: Sufism teaches people the reality of heaven and hell. Hell, according to Sufis, is where God is not. Since there is no place like that, there is no hell (pain and agony). There is no otherness, only opposites. According to Muhammad Iqbal (d. 1938),[10] heaven and hell are not two distinct places. Rather, they are two different states. Hell is not an eternal place of torture created by God, the Punisher. Rather, it is an experience similar to that of a reformatory, where a deviant servant who meets his Lord must first endure a period of reformation to become sensitive, considerate, and receptive to His renewing winds of mercy again. According to the Qur'an, the purpose of hell is for a person to understand his terrible failure as a human being.

Sufism is freedom. Real freedom is to be freed from the seductions of the ego. To simply *believe* in freedom does not render a person free; a person suffering from the burden of the ego-self (*nefis*) like a helpless slave cannot be considered free. For instance, how can anyone claim to be free when he is a slave of tobacco and unable to overcome the desire to smoke even though he wants to quit? Only a person like Diogenes (d. 323 BCE)[11] who has conquered his carnal appetite and egotistical drive – rather than becoming a slave to them – can say to Alexander the Great, "You are a slave of my slave!" and thus be considered truly free.

Sufism means unity. To be human means to unite everything. The meaning of the phrase *"La ilaha illa'Llah"* (There is no god but God) is to see that all of creation is under God's command. It is only through the command of God that all of existence reveals its essence.

In sum, we can say that Kenan Rifa'i's understanding of Sufism requires seekers to consider all of creation as the Truth and the Truth as all of creation. This perspective requires that seekers annihilate their transient beings and sacrifice the never-ending demands of the *nefis* in the service of the Eternal Truth, and, by extension, in the service of creation. Thus a true Sufi is the one

---

10. Renowned South Asian intellectual and philosopher-poet who lived in colonial India during the British Empire.

11. Diogenes of Sinope, a Greek philosopher who argued for the philosophical position of asceticism and an emphasis on ethics.

who is successful in the complete transformation of his being, so much so that he is able to approach all of existence – which humans perceive in the form of infinite particles – as a meaningful unity.

A true Sufi is a person who cherishes the life given to him by God to realize his own truth, and doesn't waste time trying to assess his own value and station. It is the person who understands that all encounters between human beings and material things belong to the realm of multiplicity, much like concentric circles formed in the water when triggered by the casting of a stone.

As stated in his book, Kenan Rifa'i says, "Sufism originally exists without the limits of any religion. Sufism is a sequence of thoughts and a life experience that begins and develops with the human being. Religion relies on the explanations and commentaries of Sufism."[12]

According to prescribed law (*Şeriat* Ar. *Shari'a*), what's mine is mine and what's yours is yours. The Sufi Path (*Tarikat*) states that yours is yours and mine is also yours. But Reality or Truth (*Hakikat*) states that neither yours is yours nor mine is mine.

A true Sufi is a person who gives this world its due by being grateful and displaying every beauty granted to him through his state. At the same time this person gives what is due to the Hereafter. Kenan Rifa'i explains this truth through the following example: "I have three pairs of glasses. One is for seeing what is near: this world. The second is for seeing what is far: the next world. With the third pair, I see both near and far, this world and the next, and these are the glasses of Sufism."[13] A true Sufi is the person who can be with the Beloved in his heart at any time, without turning away from worldly affairs for a single moment.

A true Sufi makes known the realities of this world and their inner meaning, even in what appear to be mundane events. Once a knife was lying on a dresser. Kenan Rifa'i asked what it was. Someone replied, "a knife, used specially to cut tubes," to which he said, "Why did you leave it there? Someone might cut himself by mistake," and added, "just as it is important not to leave sharp, dangerous objects lying around to avoid accidents, it is necessary to shed evil manners from your being so that the heart and spirit are not injured by them. Your body is not the proper place for such manners."

---

12. Ayverdi, *Ken'an Rifa'i*, p. 221.
13. Ibid., p. 220.

We might say that it is through the training of Sufism that we can find heaven while still in this world. Peace and happiness, which are the real heaven, lead the seeker to true freedom through the same training. From this perspective, Sufism is the path through which a human being can attain true humanity.

Chapter Two:
Principles of Conduct (*Edep*)

Q: We'd like to continue to discuss *edep*. There is a poem by Kenan Rifa'i that was published in the collection titled "*Ilahi-yyat-i-Kenan*."[1] Could you help explain it? It reads:

> Know: the spirit (*can*) of a human being's (Adam's)[2] body is *edep*;
> The heart and eye of the light of humanity is *edep*
>
> He who lacks *edep* is not a human,
> What distinguishes humanity from animals is *edep*
>
> If you wish to smash the head of Iblis[3]
> Open your eyes; what kills Iblis is *edep*
>
> Recite the verses of the Holy Qur'an
> See that its entire meaning is *edep*
>
> This is the word of the great Shams, no doubt
> What makes us acceptable to God is *edep*
>
> May God make *edep* our closest aide
> In both worlds, O Kenan, salvation is *edep*

A: Our teachers have always said that *edep* means to rise to the

---

1. Kenan Rifa'i, *Ilahiyat-ı Ken'an*, ed. Yusuf Ömürlü and Dinçer Dalkılıç (Istanbul, 1988), p. 36.
2. "Adam" has two meanings in Turkish: the first is the proper name "Adam," as in the prophet and first human; the second is the general, "human being."
3. See Glossary.

state of witnessing God's manifestation in everything. My teacher went deeper and explained *edep* as the meaning of the Perfected Human, the lover of God. *Edep* is a station that transforms an ordinary human being into a Perfected Human. Who is a Perfected Human? A Perfected Human is a king who reveals the essence of God in him; in other words, who establishes the essence of God as his spirit, and manifests the Muhammadan Reality in himself. In saying "Know: the spirit of a person's body is *edep*," my teacher is asking the following question: "the spirit in this body is *edep*, but have you given it life?" He continues, if you give it life, if you transform it to *edep*, if you cease to practice duality, and stop finding fault in everything, then you have attained the station of the Perfected Human. As Ibrahim Hakki (d. 1194/1780)[4] of Erzurum states (in his poetry), "Don't ask why it is so, it is appropriate just so," which means you must realize that everything is from God. Then you are at the station of the Perfected Human. It is only after attaining this station that a person can be trusted to distinguish between right and wrong.

The inner meaning of this can be explained through the thirty-fifth verse of the chapter of Light in the Qur'an, also called the "Light Verse": "God is the Light of the heavens and earth. His Light is like this: there is a niche, and in it a lamp, the lamp inside a glass, a glass like a glittering star, fuelled from a blessed olive tree from neither east nor west, whose oil gives light even when no fire touches it – light upon light – God guides whomever He wills to His Light; God draws such comparisons for people; God has full knowledge of everything –"[5]

In this verse, the niche in which the lamp is placed is the breast of a human. The glass is the human heart. The burning light is man's secret. As my teacher says: "the secret in Adam/the human body is *edep*." This means that the secret in the heart, which is located in the breast, which is in the body of Adam, is *edep*. The blessed tree mentioned in the verse is faith in the unseen. What does faith in the unseen mean, friends? According to 'Abd al-Karim al-Jili (d. 832/1428),[6] to have faith in the unseen is to be able to

---

4. Renowned Sufi teacher and scholar from Erzurum in eastern Anatolia.

5. Qur'an, *sura al-Nur* (Light), (24:35). Translation M. A. Abdel Haleem, *The Qur'an*, (New York: Oxford University Press, 2005), p. 223.

6. Sufi teacher and scholar from Baghdad, is remembered as one of the foremost exponents of the writings of Ibn 'Arabi.

see the Truth in creation. It is to acknowledge that the creation we think we see is not the truth and that the ultimate Truth manifesting from creation is God.

The olive tree refers to Absolute Truth. The statement that it cannot be attributed either to the east or the west demonstrates to us the necessity of steering a middle course between God's incomparability (*tenzih;* Ar. *tanzih*) and similarity (*teşbih;* Ar. *tashbih*). Let me explain this a bit further: when discussing that splendid olive tree of neither the east nor the west, do not lean towards complete transcendence or immanence. Stand on a ground in between the two. What does this tell us? Transcendence means seeing God as above everything. He is so sublime that His meaning cannot be reached or encompassed; He owns everything. We know this; so, learn and know this well. This is *tenzih*. However, at the same time, God makes Himself manifest through His creation in a state of similarity, and we call this *teşbih*. Namely, His names, attributes, and actions are manifested through humans, who we think we can fully see. This is *teşbih*. When we understand both *tenzih* and *teşbih* of God, and say "God is the Most High and Sublime, but He is also manifest in His creation," then we are on the middle path between *tenzih* and *teşbih*. At this stage, God says, your olive tree – which ignites your internal fire such that your latent *edep* is made apparent – becomes visible to your sight. When that olive tree becomes visible and begins to shower its light, you become light upon light, which is comparable to the prevalence of *edep*. God's words also suggest that you possess a certain light, but it is in a dormant state; it becomes manifest, becoming light upon light. But know well that all this only occurs with God's will and permission. Nothing else can trigger such a major transformation in you. In saying "Know: the spirit of a person's body is *edep*," what my teacher tries to convey is that the station of "light upon light" is the manifestation of *edep* from you. We should also know that the meaning of our "eye" in the verse, or the inner meaning of this seeing is *edep* as well. It is *edep* that has turned into pure light. My teacher says that when our sight is endowed with this pure light, the eye of our heart (the eye of meaning, *gönül*) opens and we start seeing the truth of everything. He also stresses that a person with no *edep* cannot be considered a real human being. Their existence is limited to the material plane. In sum, the essential quality of humanness is in *edep*.

Q: What does it mean to be a human?

A: Sura *Yasin*[7] explains what it means to be a real human being. The person who passes the farthest lote tree (*sidre münteha;* Ar. *sidrat al-muntaha*) is the person who leaves their intellect behind, who transcends all time and place with their love, and who turns to their reason to serve creation – this is an *insan*. I don't know if we will ever reach that stage, but I do know this much, that we must spare no effort in striving to be human beings, at the very least in the lexical meaning of the term. We must try to be individuals who have proactive, positive relationships with everyone; otherwise, we will only be physically human (*beşer;* Ar. *bashar*) – although my teacher goes as far as to say that to only be physically human is to be an animal. As he recalls, this is because what distinguishes Adam and human beings from animals is *edep*. If you want to destroy the station of Iblis, you must hold fast to your *edep* which allows you to kill your Iblis, your I-ness, and to respectfully bow down to that which manifests in everyone (Iblis and Satan are not the same station. Iblis is a more horrific station. Satan tries to lead you astray toward evil, whereas Iblis is what makes you say "I" and goads you into regarding yourself as better than everything else).

Q: So how did Iblis become Iblis?

A: Iblis became Iblis because he did not obey Adam. In other words, he did not believe in the unseen. He was not able to discern the divine manifestation in Adam. He said, "I am from fire and he is from clay." Do you know the difference between earth and fire? Earth has humility, lowliness, and nothingness. You spit and defecate on it, you bury your dead in it, but it never ceases to give you back in abundance; it presents you with all kinds of plants, flowers, and food. By contrast, fire is imbued with awe, haughtiness, and burning. Iblis said, "I am of fire, so I am haughty and awe-inspiring!" But Adam said, "I don't exist, I am in need of forgiveness, I am a sinner." Then God manifested Himself in the "non-existent one" (Adam), and God commanded the angels to prostrate before him. Iblis said, "I am an angel of God and the teacher of all the angels. Why should I prostrate myself before Adam?" Iblis didn't accept that Adam was God's manifestation of Lordship. In sura *Yasin*, he became an accursed outcast that was discredited, eventually mani-

---

7. Qur'an, chapter 36.

festing himself in those people who claim to have faith in God but do not acknowledge the Messenger of God. When this happened, Iblis was cast out of God's presence. If we fail to acknowledge that God's meaning becomes manifest in human beings, we become the Iblises of our time and are cast out of Adamhood, God forbid.

Q: So, was Iblis cast out because he failed to see the reality of Adam in whom God's names and attributes were manifest?

A: The manifestation of perfection can only be apparent in nothingness and the world is the only opportunity for that; Iblis was not able to perceive this. Farid al-Din 'Attar (d. 627/1230), a great figure and one of the teachers of Mevlana Rumi, presents this question: "Would you take on the duty of Iblis? That poor creature accepted it despite the cost." It was a duty and he accepted it. My teacher stresses that to be human is to refuse to comply with Iblis; to obey him is to give up one's humanity.

To continue with the poem, referring to the line, "Recite the verses of the Holy Qur'an, notice that its entire meaning is *edep*," my teacher says: "Read! If you understood the meaning of the Qur'an, as you read it, you would see that all of its meaning is *edep*. The entire meaning of the Qur'an is the Perfected Human (*al-insan al-kamil*), and the meaning of the Perfected Human is *edep*." He then reminds us of the words of Shams,[8] the great teacher of Mevlana: "What makes us acceptable to God and what makes Him pleased with us is *edep*; it is to see God's names and attributes in everything and everyone and not to be upset." My teacher ends this beautiful poem with a supplication: "May God grant us *edep*," and "*edep* leads to salvation in both worlds."

Q: Are there any other definitions of *edep*?

A: *Edep* is to witness God's oneness in everything. Say for example, that somebody is lying to you, and you are aware that they are lying. Since that person is the recipient of the name "liar," *edep* requires us to avoid that person, not to confront them about their errors, nor to revile them. *Edep* is to know that good and evil are both from God; it is to not interfere in matters, physically or verbally, knowing that everything is from God. You might question this and ask, "As people or seekers of *edep*, are we never to inter-

---

8. Shams-i Tabrizi.

fere?" To this I would say, if we witness actions that pose a threat to the survival of our country and state, or are against established precepts of morality and God's commandments, the Şeriat, then we have the right to object three times. However, each time we must raise our objection within the limits designated by edep, all the while taking great care not to break the person's heart or upset them. This is how our teachers always dealt with our mistakes. It is a wonderful God-given gift to be crowned with edep! Our beloved master the Prophet said: "My Lord gave me my manners and He indeed made them perfect." Another relevant point is that edep is beautiful conduct. Edep leads to beautiful conduct. As you know, the Holy Prophet has been sent to complete the beauty of conduct. According to one saying of Muhammad (hadith), he says, "This is the house of beautiful conduct. As the last of the prophets, I put the final brick in its place and 'Ali[9] explained its meaning." My teacher expresses the same view, saying, "Edep is a crown made from divine light. If you wear it, you will be safe wherever you go." If a person does not get angry, sad, or upset and does not perceive anything or anyone as an enemy, then who or what can do any harm to them?

There is a story about this that I like very much. There was a friend of God (veli; Ar. wali)[10] – an endearing man – who earned his living by painting houses. One day he accepted a job that required him to work with an extremely arrogant family. They repeatedly harassed and threatened him, saying, "We won't pay you if we don't like the results." They gave him a hard time by complaining for no reason about the exact color of the shades. It is no surprise that the person who had introduced him to the family got very upset with them; at the same time he was amazed at the painter's indifference in the face of this cruel abuse. He said to him, "You taught us to make the distinction between good and evil, but you yourself didn't object to anything they said even though the treatment you were subjected to was wrong!" The wise painter replied, "My son, you are right; I should have objected at least verbally. But so thoroughly has my heart learnt that everything is from God that my tongue just conformed."

Husam al-Din Arzanjani was a great debater. Before he began

---

9. See Glossary.

10. I have rendered the term wali "friend of God" in some instances, and simply "saint" in others.

frequenting the gatherings of dervishes and spending time with them, he would ignite controversies everywhere he went. In addition to his role as an arbitrator, he was also an extremely eloquent speaker. But after spending time with dervishes, his desire to debate with others diminished and lost its previous appeal.[11]

We see that *edep* is something that can even silence the tongue from time to time. It settles in a person's heart and keeps them at peace. *Edep* is such a state. My teacher says that Sufism is *edep*. *Edep* can lead to the furthest station of *"La mawjuda illa'Llah,"* (except God nothing exists). Given this, *edep* elevates a person to such an extent that they even begin to respect seemingly inanimate objects. How is it possible to respect inanimate things? By not hitting or breaking them, and not pushing aside a hastily removed article of clothing with your leg. It is to respect your pets and the animals around you; in short, to respect the entire fauna and flora as much as you respect the people you love and care for. A very dear Sufi friend of mine from Switzerland once told me that she would ask her plants and flowers for their permission whenever she wanted to plant another flower in the same spot, saying, "You'll be sharing your nourishment; will you allow me to plant a sibling next to you?" Honestly, this is the reality of it.

The world is the Qur'an, and we revere our scripture in its entirety. We kiss it, press it against our foreheads, and don't touch it unless we have performed ablution. But the Qur'an has words like Pharaoh, Satan and names of evil people who persecuted the messengers. Do we tear some pages out because they contain the names of those wicked people? Similarly, to have *edep* is to not feel any grudge or hatred against people sent to us by God – even in the form of Pharaoh – and to always remember that each and every thing exists for a reason. When we consider *edep* from this perspective, all things will appear as lovely and beautiful.

Edep is of two types: outer *edep* and inner *edep*. Outer *edep* entails the carrying out of God's basic commandments in the form of dos and don'ts. The goal of outer *edep* is to eliminate reason when performing outward duties ordained by God. This is to say, I must fulfill the duty that is incumbent on me even though I might not fully understand it. This is one of the implications of outer *edep* in the presence of God. Inner *edep* is the final station for a person

---

11. See Rumi's *Fihi Ma Fihi,* discourse 39.

who has observed his external duties perfectly. It is the station of witnessing the manifestations of the Truth in everyone and everything. This is the real meaning of what it means to be Muslim. We proclaim, "*Ashhadu an la ilaha illa'Llah*" (I testify that there is no god but God). We do not say, "I know" or "I believe." To testify something, one has to have witnessed it. So a person endowed with inner *edep* has reached the station of beholding or witnessing. Abraham had such an esteemed station that the Greatest Shaykh Muhiyuddin Ibn 'Arabi (d. 638/1240) calls it the "station of excessive love of God," the "station of contentment," and the "station of trustworthiness." How did Abraham reach the station of "except God, nothing exists"? By first recognizing that the things he was worshipping would disappear. "I cannot worship that which sets and vanishes," he said. Don't we also worship things that will eventually set and vanish? Like our children, spouse, money, clothes, education, knowledge? Abraham left all these things behind. "There is only You, it is You Who is manifest in everything" he said. His loyalty to God was so robust that he agreed to sacrifice his son for His sake. This is the station of contentment and trustworthiness: "I am so fully satisfied with you O God, I am certain to the point of never turning back!" he said. And God, in turn, answered with the gift of four stations:

First, Abraham had asked that the Prophet Muhammad be born from his offspring. "O God," he prayed, "make me the antecedent of this truth which I have witnessed." His prayer was granted.

Second, God raised him to such a station that he was even prepared to sacrifice his son for God.

Third, despite his complete knowledge that everything is from God, he never gave up in his struggle against Nimrod. This teaches us that we must differentiate between right and wrong and struggle against wrong, but in our hearts we must not look down on it. Rather we must be able to see the reflection of oneness in it.

Fourth, God favored Abraham by blessing him with the duty of building the Sacred House of God, the Ka'ba, which is the embodiment of this meaning. Abraham was the first human being to complete the building of the Ka'ba.

The thirty-seventh verse of the Chapter of Abraham says, "Our Lord, I have established some of my offspring in an uncultivated valley, close to Your Sacred House, Lord, so that they may keep up the prayer. Make people's hearts turn to them, and provide them with produce, so that they may be thankful.”[12]

In the fortieth verse, it is said, “Lord, grant that I and my off-spring may keep up the prayer. Our Lord, accept my request.”[13]

Q: What is the meaning of building the Ka'ba?

A: It is actually quite fitting that Abraham was entrusted to build the Ka'ba. It was not a coincidence. From among the Prophets, Abraham was the first to make his heart a Ka'ba. That is, he purified his heart of everything other than God, transforming his heart into the Ka'ba that reflected and radiated his God. God also valued Abraham's heart and commanded him to “display his heart publicly so people could circumambulate it.” It was Adam who placed the first stone of its foundation, but it was Abraham who made it into a house. Did the hearts of men not fill up with idols afterwards? Yes, they did, until the time of the Prophet Muhammad; the transformation of the Ka'ba into a place completely free of idols then took place with the Muhammadan Şeriat of Islam. For this reason, Islam is the highest station and 'Ali is the one who broke the idols.

As you know, in order to break the idols the Prophet Muhammad entered the Ka'ba with 'Ali and said to 'Ali: “Climb on my shoulders O 'Ali. You will break the idols because you occupy the station of *murshid* (spiritual guide). You will break the idols in the hearts of people; the meaning of your being will smash all the idols in people's hearts.” This is the message of the Prophet to him. 'Ali, however, shrank away from doing so, saying, “I cannot step on your shoulders! My *edep* prevents me from doing so!” But the Prophet insisted: “O 'Ali! The order (of a *murshid*) prevails over *edep* (*Ya 'Ali! al-amr fawq al-adab*).” So 'Ali stepped onto the Prophet's shoulders. Looking down from this exalted station, he saw the blessed feet of the Prophet everywhere. At eye-level he saw the chest of the Prophet, and when he looked to the sky, he saw the face and beauty of the Prophet, which is to say that the Prophet's meaning manifested as God's beauty. Everybody said, “O 'Ali, you are the only person who can see this meaning (of God's Messenger).” This is why, in a famous *hadith*, the Prophet said, “There is nobody who knows 'Ali save God and myself. There is nobody who knows me save God and 'Ali. And there is nobody who knows God save myself and 'Ali.”

---

12. Qur'an, sura Abraham (14:37). Tr. Haleem, *Qur'an*, p. 161.
13. Qur'an, sura Abraham (14:40). *Ibid.*

Q: Kenan Rifaʻi drew a comparison between the human heart and a garden, and between the spiritual guide and the gardener. Which negative qualities need to be cleansed and removed in order for *edeb* to manifest in the heart?

A: Every rational human being has an eight-part garden in his/her heart. Just like a gardener who has taken on for himself the maintenance of a garden, and who weeds, tends and cultivates the garden, my teacher reminds us that we human beings should rid our flower beds of the ugly grass and weeds with which they are overgrown.

The first garden is the garden of unicity. Unicity, or *tevhid*, is to establish the oneness of God and to see the manifestations of Truth in everything and everyone. He says, "if the heart has grown the weeds of dualism, of associating partners with God (*shirk*), and of valuing created things more than God, it is necessary to uproot those weeds." By the way, we must never forget that the real hidden *shirk* is our love for ourselves. The purpose of all knowledge is *tevhid*; when this is attained, it is evident that the person who only acquires worldly knowledge exerts effort and energy in vain.

The second garden is the garden of having complete trust in God (*tevekkül*; Ar. *tawakkul*). It is to realize that nobody holds any power over anything except God. Until this is understood, you cannot say, "I have complete trust in God." You must remove every thorn of fear and worry from this garden. Can a person who has understood that everything is from God have anything to fear? Whom else would they turn to for help and whom else would they seek to endear themselves to?

The third garden is the garden of entrustment (*tefviz*; Ar. *tafwid*). It is to hand yourself over to the Will of God in such perfect compliance that all the weeds and thorns of self-reliance, individual will, and personal desires have to be removed. We must give ourselves over completely to His will and tie the tiny boats of our relative being to God's boat. We don't always understand that the place that He takes us to is the right place. It should be clear that *tefviz* does not mean that we stop taking precautions. We take precautions. We struggle to take precautions. We struggle and work hard. But we remain aware that the outcome will be in our favor, whether it is what we are striving for or not.

The fourth garden is the garden of patience (*sabir*) and it is divided into four types of patience. The first type of patience is what we need to face the difficulties that confront us on the path of servitude to the Truth. That is, for when we try to sense our nothingness, and realize our servitude. Suppose someone insults us with a volley of expletives and treats us with utter contempt. The first level of patience in this instance is the ability to welcome the situation, saying, "O God! I am a servant. In order to demonstrate my servitude, I need this person, so I am grateful for him!" The second type of patience is the ability to refrain from worldly pleasures. It means acknowledging the fact that the things we aspire to are all transient, such as wealth, possessions, physical beauty, intelligence, knowledge and ideas. The third type of patience is the struggle to resist the desire to possess worldly things. The fourth is the patience to endure trouble, disaster and difficulty. This is the highest level of patience. True praise is patience. "Allah is with those who are patient."[14]

The fifth garden is contentment (*rıza*; Ar. *rida*). How sublime a station is contentment! It is to ask neither to be granted a particular blessing, nor to be delivered from punishment or the troubles (that He tests us with). Rather, it is to accept things as they are and not show any displeasure, nor feel any resentment. One day a man walked up to my teacher and said, "May God be content with you!" My teacher replied, "Well, first let me be content with Him!" Baffled, the man asked, "What do you mean, sir?" My teacher replied, "First I, without complaint, should be content with everything He has given me, and then He will be content with me." Indeed, he was a perfect model of contentment with God. When he had great difficulty speaking due to frequent coughing fits, my mother, who was one of his students, said to him, "Won't you please pray for God to relieve you of this cough so you can teach us more comfortably? Your prayers are not rejected." He answered, "How can I treat a guest from my God with displeasure? If I do, it will complain about me to God. It is my guest and I try to host my guests beautifully." This is what it means to be at the station of contentment.

After the garden of contentment is the sixth garden, the garden of divine knowledge (*marifet*; Ar. *ma'rifa*). This is unveiled when contentment has been attained as a person's general state. People of divine knowledge have stripped themselves of everything other

---

14. A common Qur'anic refrain, found in sura *al-Baqara* (the Cow), (2:153) and several other verses.

than God. They do not incline towards anything except God. They become people of beautiful conduct, who are patient, content, trusting, and in submission. They are endowed with *marifet* and awaken others. In other words, they are the people of service. They teach and show people through their own service and states that everything is the Truth.

The seventh garden is that of love (*muhabbet;* Ar. *mahabba*). It is the station of not preferring anything to the passionate and compassionate love for God.[15] It is the smashing of idols of the *nefis*: children, worldly power, rank, and possessions.

When it comes to the eighth garden, my teacher says, "It is wisdom (*hikmet;* Ar. *hikma*); it is to be truthful in your words, actions, and wishes." Wisdom is what is spoken by people of gnosis. Such people only speak the truth. They reveal the truth of what we assume to be wrong. No one can object to their words because they are endowed with the knowledge, vision and insight to persuade anyone. Since in their speech they only speak about God, nothing ugly or negative issues forth from them.

The gardener enters these gardens and waters all the flowers and trees with the water of divine knowledge (*ilm-i ledün;* Ar. *al-'ilm al-laduni*). In this way, it becomes the spirit in the spirit. In other words, it becomes, "Know: the spirit in the human being/Adam's body is beautiful conduct."

Shibli (d. 334/945)[16] said, "My Lord taught me *edep* through three events." His students asked him about those events. He said, "A woman came to me. Her husband had been enamored with another woman and eventually left her in the lurch. She was in complete disarray; dispirited and disheveled. In desperation, she pleaded, 'Please find me my husband! I beg you! They call you a great lover of God; I beseech you to return him to me!' In an effort to bring her back to a proper state, I said, 'O woman, pull yourself together; cover your hair, regain your composure, and come back to me in decent appearance.' Shocked, she said to me, 'O Good Lord! My love for my husband prevents me from realizing what

---

15. "*Aşk*" is rendered here "passionate love" and "*muhabbet*" as "compassionate love." In doing this, I follow Carl Ernst's distinction of the two terms. See Ernst "Ruzbihan Baqli on Love as 'Essential Desire'," in A. Geise and Johann Christoph Burgel, *God is Beautiful and He Loves Beauty: Festschrift for Annemarie Schimmel*, (Berlin: Peter Lang, 1994), p. 182.

16. Abu Bakr al-Shibli was an important Sufi and a disciple of Junayd Baghdadi.

condition I am in, but how is it that you notice my hair and clothing, when you claim to be a lover of God?' I learnt a serious lesson from this. The second event involved a boy. I lit a candle and asked the boy where the light of the candle comes from. He smiled, blew out the candle and answered, 'It comes from wherever it has gone.' The third event had to do with a drunkard. He was staggering in the dirt, on the verge of falling at any moment. I cautioned him, 'O my son, why do you drink so much? You will fall and become dirty!' Despite his highly drunken state, he replied, 'O great Shibli! If I fall into the mud, a bucket of water suffices to wash me clean. But you saw a fault in me. If you fall from your current station, nothing can cleanse you!' He said, 'that is how I learnt the meaning of real *edep*.'" He was a great master of *edep*. Through such beauty, they teach us the meaning of *edep*.

Q: Can you speak about the *edep* of the Prophet?

A: The Prophet was the humblest of men, because all the blessings of both worlds were collected in him. Naturally, he was the most humble, more than anybody else.

No one was able to say *salam* (give greetings) before the Prophet. No one ever said *salam* before him because he would always act first and say *salam*. Even if he was not saying *salam* explicitly, he was still extremely humble. He was the one who would begin the conversation. It was from him that people heard and learnt how to give greetings. People who have come and gone, whatever they have and don't have, everything is thanks to him, and all things are his shadows. When the shadow of a person enters his house before him, what has really entered the house is the owner of the shadow. Although the shadow appears to have entered first and preceded the owner, it is only a derivative of the owner.

Now this *edep* was not something new that came with Muhammad, and was not particular to his time. The Muhammadan character has been present since the time of Adam, inherent in everyone, in every cell. However, in the cells of some, the manifestation of this character is illuminated, in some it is half illuminated, and in some it is dark. The illumination of this character in people, even if it appears now, is a feature that belongs to pre-eternity. This pre-eternal light is inherent in everyone; one ray of that light in a human being renders them more pure, more illuminated and more humble as compared to all other beings.

When the time came for our Prophet to repeat the ascension (*mirac*; Ar. *mi'raj*)[17] that he had experienced in pre-eternal time, before undertaking this journey into himself, he displayed his *edep* through patience. He was bleeding all over. They had thrown a feces-filled udder (of a she-camel) on his head. They ridiculed him so much. Yet, when he raised his hands, he cried to his God, "They don't know You, O God! They can't recognize You! Please forgive them for they cannot see You! Forgive them. It is You that I see in them." That night, the Prophet was given the *mirac*. It was no other than the revelation and the unveiling of his own mysteries and meanings to himself. This is how Ibn 'Arabi recounted it.

Sura *al-Najm*[18] (The Star) speaks about the Prophet's ascension beautifully. He was first carried to Jerusalem by Buraq,[19] which was the Prophet's patience. It always puzzled me why the Prophet, who made every "where" one, went to Jerusalem first; what was he trying to teach us by going there? I always wondered about this. Then, during a visit to Jerusalem, I saw the stone on which Abraham laid his son Ishmael (Isma'il) to sacrifice. Only then did I understand that he was trying to give us a message. He was telling us, "If you want to live your ascension, and if you want to reach your truth (*hakikat*), first set foot on the platform of patience, and submit yourself." That is, "Be Islam." Submission is Islam. The word Islam comes from the word *teslim* (Ar. *taslim*) - submission. Peace and presence are also Islam. That is to say, the one who submits receives peace and presence. From there, the Prophet continued his ascension with patience. He passed through all the levels of paradise; at each level he met with a messenger of God. He met Abraham at the highest station of paradise. One level lower, he met Moses.

Moses is at the rank of the Prophet's intellect. God had given him the command, "Take off your sandals."[20] That is, if you want to reach Him, you have to get rid of your shoes (symbolizing the entice-

___

17. Reference is to the Prophet Muhammad's night journey (*isra'*) from Mecca to Jerusalem, which was followed by his ascension (*mi'raj*) to heaven. He is said to have first been led by the Angel Gabriel, before proceeding himself in the final stage to the closest possible proximity to God.

18. Qur'an, sura *al-Najm* (the Star) 53.

19. Buraq refers to the steed on which Muhammad is said to have been carried from Mecca to Jerusalem and thereon to heaven, during the episode known as the *mi'raj* (ascension).

20. Reference to Qur'an sura *Ta-Ha* (20:12), "I am your Lord. Take off your sandals: you are in the sacred valley of Tuwa."

ments of this world and the next). It is as if Moses told Muhammad, "Leave me; leave your intellect and go." And when they reached the Lotus Tree at the Furthest End, the intellect, or Angel Gabriel said, "I can't go any further." The Prophet ascended after leaving his intellect, the Angel Gabriel, who had guided him there, and was most possibly his spiritual guide (*murshid*) (thus even leaving behind his *murshid*). The Prophet ascended through his love and the attribute of sainthood that had been granted to him in pre-eternity. But it wasn't without a severe test that he ascended. God placed before him all that had been and was to be created. Everything was out in the open – that which is alive now, that which once lived, and that which will live – all were open before him in their true meaning. God said, "O my beloved! I have created all this for you. You are my reality. You don't exist; you are nothing. For this reason, I have created everything for you. I will give all of this to you now if you ask." The Prophet, who is the greatest servant at the station of *edep*, said, "I want you, O Lord, I want you!" This wish elevated him even higher. He reached the station of absolute unicity (*ahadiyet* Ar. *ahadiyya*), or as Ibn 'Arabi explains, it is like the coming together of two ends of a bow. Or more precisely, when the Prophet in utmost bewilderment asked, "Where am I?" God spoke to him, "Place your right foot over the left. See that you are in Me." In that state of oneness, our Prophet sensed his status as servant and made supplications in our favor, so that we would understand its meaning. Perhaps if he had not remembered us at that moment, we would have never known that meaning.

The station of Mahmud (praised) is the highest station; it is the station of being thankful and giving praise. The *edep* of the Prophet is conveyed in sura *Najm*: "By the star when it sets! Your companion has not strayed; he is not deluded; he does not speak from his own desire. The Qur'an is nothing less than a revelation that is sent to him.... His sight never wavered, nor was it too bold, and he saw some of the greatest signs of his Lord."[21] The Prophet

---

21. The complete verse is: "By the star when it sets! Your companion has not strayed; he is not deluded; he does not speak from his own desire. The Qur'an is nothing less than a revelation that is sent to him. It was taught to him by [an angel] with mighty powers and great strength, who stood on the highest horizon and then approached – coming down until he was two bow-lengths away or even closer – and revealed to God's servant what He revealed. [The Prophet's] own heart did not distort what he saw. Are you going to dispute with him what he saw

is he on whose name we can take an oath. God's meaning becomes manifest from him. Do you see how our discussion began, and how it now ends at the same place? The meaning of the chapter of Light (sura *Nur*) is the manifestation of *edep* in the Prophet. May God grant us that *edep*.

Q: You said earlier that the meaning of *edep* is "*La ilaha illa'Llah*" (There is no god but God).

A: We know that *edep* is the foundation of religion, the essence of what it means to be human, and the meaning that illuminates the heart. Human beings have to be infused with *edep*. When the *nefis* falls deeply in love with the spirit (*ruh*) such that everything it perceives becomes the spirit, it takes the spirit as its lord and agrees to come under its complete guidance. When this love reaches its greatest height, with the coming together of the *nefis* with the *ruh*, at that time the person becomes *edep*. So *edep* here means to see the oneness of the Truth wherever one looks. Sufis call this the station of "the unicity of God" (*vahdaniyet*; Ar. *wahdaniyya*), which means to see the Truth in multiplicity. At this point *La ilaha illa'Llah* (There is no god but God) becomes *la mawjuda illa'Llah* (except God nothing exists). In reality, there is no being that exists alongside God. When this is understood, it becomes clear that the whole world is the Qur'an. Since the world is the Qur'an and we should not touch the Qur'an without performing ablution (or being in state of ritual purity), similarly we should not look scornfully at any manifestation of God that exists in the world.

To understand this, consider the creation of human beings. Why do we have to unite all manifestation? Why is it necessary to unite the attributes of Majesty (*celal*; Ar. *jalal*) and Beauty (*cemal* Ar. *jamal*) of Truth? Approaching it from this perspective alerts us to two Qur'anic verses: first, from sura *Ya-Sin*: "Can they not see how, among the things made by Our hands, We have created the livestock that they control?"[22] "Livestock" in this verse refers to soft animal. People interpret this to mean sheep, so it is as if God

---

with his own eyes? A second time he saw him: by the lote tree beyond which none may pass near the Garden of Restfulness, when the tree was covered in nameless [splendour]. His sight never wavered, nor was it too bold, and he saw some of the greatest signs of his Lord. Qur'an, *al-Najm* (the Star), (53:1-18). Tr. Haleem, *Qur'an*, p. 347.

22. Qur'an, *Ya-Sin*, (36:71). Tr. Haleem, *Qur'an*, p.284.

says "We created many sheep; how are humans benefiting from them?" It can also mean that once the animal is consumed, it becomes part of the human being, and hence acquires the capacity to obtain spiritual knowledge. But let's try to find a deeper meaning. By "things made by Our hands," God means human beings who are created with the attributes of Majesty and Beauty. God says, "We have softened the *nefis* in man – the station of animality – and caused soft and beneficial animals to come forth from it. With Our attributes of Majesty and Beauty, We have turned the *nefis* into a useful animal that comes under the dominion of the serving spirit. The *nefis*, annihilated in its love, considers the spirit its master."

Q: What does it mean to be taught by Majesty and Beauty?

A: To be taught by Majesty refers to God's teaching us through affliction and challenge, or things that appear to us as such when in reality they are not. "Majesty," in reality, is God's will and blessing. It is God's manifestation on earth. Look at the earth; when God manifests, the earth shakes and quivers from the encounter. Similarly, when the earth that is the body encounters God's manifestation there is an earthquake. This is Majesty. Beauty on the other hand, is teaching through gentleness, softness, generosity, and beautiful things. Both (Majesty and Beauty) are necessary and of immense importance. Nothing in the world is trivial or in vain. Things may only appear as such from the outside. For instance, a woman washing clothes by a river first beats the clothes with a hammer, then spreads them over the bushes to dry, then folds and collects them. Beating, wetting and drying are all distinct actions and opposites of each other, but the goal is the same – to clean the clothes and make them worthy of being adorned by the beautiful body.

In the *Fihi Ma Fihi*,[23] Mevlana Rumi says, "They beat a carpet with a stick to dust it. People of reason don't call this scolding. But when they beat a loved one or their child, they call it a beating, or a scolding, though it is the manifestation love." When we want to clean our clothes, we first dip them in water. Then we dry them. But why do we wet the thing that we will dry soon after? Why do we choose to clean it in this way? Because there is no other way to clean. If God only "dried" us, we wouldn't become clean

23. A collection of Rumi's discourses, conversations, and commentaries on various topics. For an English translation, see *Signs of the Unseen: The Discourses of Jalaluddin Rumi*, Wheeler Thackston, (Shambhala, 1999).

so sometimes He "moistens" us. That is, sometimes He teaches us through pain, sorrow and hardship. If we confront these with grace, we reach a state of inner peace. This peace is Beauty. God first moistens, and then dries us in order that we become thoroughly cleansed. As a result of these treatments from God, human beings soften and subdue their egotistical desires and wishes and transform them into beneficial abilities. This is a blessing derived from these processes, since human beings then disseminate subtle blessings.

God said to Iblis: "Iblis, what prevents you from bowing down to the man I have made with My own hands?"[24] This and the previous verse we mentioned[25] complement each other; God refers to humans when He mentions the thing created with His two hands. Everything *except* the human being has been created with one hand because human beings, like angels, can manifest the attributes of Beauty, or like satans and the angels of torment, can manifest the attributes of Majesty. Human beings unite these in themselves, thereby uniting the two seas while at the same time preventing them from merging with one another, like a passage that bridges paths together.[26] In their inner aspects human beings are like their Lord, but in their outer aspects they are servants. The human being is an image derived from humanness and the Truth. With respect to rank (*mertebe;* Ar. *martaba*), the human being, who possesses qualities of Lordship, is purer than all other creation. At the same time, as the possessor of qualities of servitude, there is no creation lower than the human being. Therefore God's beautiful attributes manifest in the human being. The heart of the human being carries the beautiful spirit and majestic self. The two are separated by the isthmus (*barzakh*) of intellect just like the two seas that don't merge with the *barzakh*. The Qur'anic verses we mentioned above confirm that the human being has been created with Beauty and Majesty. We are not supposed to get angry or upset by Majesty or

---

24. Qur'an, *Sad,* (38:75). Tr. Haleem, *Qur'an,* p. 293.

25. "Can they not see how, among the things made by Our hands, We have created the livestock that they control?" Qur'an, *Ya-Sin,* (36:71). Tr. Haleem, *Qur'an,* p.284.

26. The reference is to the Qur'anic verse: "It is He Who released the two bodies of flowing water, one sweet and fresh and the other salty and bitter, and put an insurmountable barrier between them." Qur'an, *al-Furqan* (the Differentiator), (25:53). Tr. Haleem, *Qur'an,* p. 230.

to become too content with Beauty. Rather, to know Majesty and Beauty as one is also *edep*. What is *edep*? It is perfection (*kemal*), like the hadith where the Prophet said, "My Lord taught me *edep* and made my *edep* beautiful." So, anyone without *edep* is also without divine blessings. May God grant us the *edep* of this world and that of the next.

> Q: This raises a very important question. If all things are the Truth and a manifestation of God's Names, then why is there punishment for those who do evil?

A: God Almighty has opposing names. For instance, He has names that give glory and honor, and He has names that abase, cause misery, and lowliness. He is the Guide (*Hadi*), who leads His servants on the straight path and gives them success with perfect goodness; at the same time He is the Misguider (*muzil*; Ar. *mudil*) who leads astray. He forgives His servants to the extent that they will not be responsible for any wrong they committed, but He is also the Avenger (*müntakim*; Ar. *muntaqim*) who takes revenge, and as the Just He delivers the punishments that His servants deserve (on account of their sins). These names belong to God; He possesses all these names. The names requested God, "O Lord! Grant us a place to manifest so that the meaning of these names can be realized."

One should not say, "I didn't get to choose these parents," or "I didn't ask for these qualities," or "why did I come into this world?" This is because each individual knows his name from the time of pre-eternity. And a person's name longs to perfect itself and to be reunited with God. So it tries to acquire a physical body. To this end, it chooses its own family and path. Eventually, the human being comes to this world. And if a person commits an atrocity, he is confronted by the name "the Avenger." That is, opposite names punish each other in this world. So if you do something negative to another person, you are made to face the name "Avenger." God manifests Himself on things equally, but everyone benefits from Him according to his abilities. This is no different from God doing as He wishes. Every thing that is done by God is rooted in wisdom. It is part of His wisdom to manifest to each thing in accordance with their ability. So if it is appropriate for someone to be shown mercy, He does not take revenge on him. Similarly, He does not show mercy on anyone who is to be punished. Doing otherwise goes against His wisdom. "Pharaoh said, 'Moses, who is this Lord of yours?' Moses replied, 'Our Lord is He who endowed all things with a destiny in accordance with their creation; the enactment of that destiny became for them the Straight Path to which they were guided.'"[27]

Q: So everybody's "guidance" refers to their immutable entities (*ayan-ı sabite*; Ar. *a'yan al-thabit*)?

A: Yes, but let's explain this further since we have gone too deep. In the realm of Unicity, that is, in the realm of "There was only I, and nothing was with Me," the foundation, essence, and immutable entities of all creation – that which has already been created and is yet to be created – was present in the entirety of God. The immutable entities of everything were present in that whole. Then Unicity manifested, giving way to multiplicity. In the former realm the immutable entities were one and the same in appearance; here they became clad in the robe of multiplicity. The image was one, but it separated into multiplicity. There, our Preserved Tablet (*levh-i mahfuz*; Ar. *al-lawh al-mahfuz*),[28] our essence, just like a pomegranate, manifested. Like this, our coming to this world was in accordance with the Preserved Tablet. Whatever there was in our pre-eternity, we have come to this world only to return to that state again. God blessed us with a body, and in addition to that body, he granted us various predispositions in this world in order for the Preserved Tablet to manifest. He brought us to this world not only with our names, which were granted in pre-eternity, but also with their opposites. These opposite names exist for our training (*terbiye*; Ar. *tarbiyya*). Bad is disciplined with good. Good is disciplined with bad. This is a manifestation of God's justice, greatness, and beauty.

Q: You have said that every created thing received a name of God. Can we discuss this further?

A: What we have been discussing is from Ibn 'Arabi's *Bezels of Wisdom* (*Fusus al-Hikam*), which is a complex work. If you ask me, "what is punishment (*ceza*; Ar. *jaza'*)?" I would say it means reciprocation. The human being is first punished in this world because whoever has done an atom's weight of good shall see it, and whoever has

---

27. The reference is to Qur'an, *Ta Ha* (20:49-50): "Our Lord is He who gave everything its form, then gave it guidance." Tr. Haleem, *Qur'an*, p. 198.
28. See Glossary.

done an atom's weight of evil shall see it as well.[29] Human beings must live in this world; that is, a person enters heaven or hell while still in this world. What does all this mean? It means that if you can't find heaven here-and-now, you can't possibly find it in the Hereafter! So what then is hell?

Let us take an example. For a quick-tempered person to live with a patient person in the same house is hell. Opposite names came to this world to discipline each other. If love manifests and people begin to accept each other gracefully, then beauty manifests, and heaven can be found in this world. On the other hand, a person's disposition can exhaust him to the extent that his life literally becomes a living hell. If this happens it is unfortunate because that person leaves the world without attaining the real goal. So again, it is through opposite names and qualities that we are taught and disciplined.

In line with God's divine wisdom, He grants people things in proportion to their abilities, as circumscribed in their Preserved Tablet, and proportional to their immutable entities. He guides them on the straight path in accordance with their abilities. So the statement, "everything becomes the projection of a particular divine name," means that that particular name fulfills its designated task in accordance with its meaning. This is captured in the following story: When a group of people took a donkey to heaven, it hee-hawed continuously. When they took it to hell it did the same thing. They said to themselves, "this creature doesn't know what heaven or hell is, so how are we supposed to reward or punish it?" One of them said, "Its punishment has already been given. It is a donkey; that is enough of a punishment."

Q: So, the binding offer (*teklif*) made in the Qur'an, the offer of *edep*, is for those who are capable of seeing the truth, not for those who are deaf and blind to it. Is this correct?

A: Yes. It is indeed impossible for a person to see the truth from the first station of the *nefis,* which we call "the commanding soul (*emmare;* Ar. *ammara*)." Who is doing the commanding here? If a person says, "I am superior to everyone. There is no one greater than me!" then the truth is veiled from him. This is his punishment. The responsibility lies with those who understand. For

---

29. This is a reference to Qur'an, sura *Zalzalah* (Earthquake), (99:7-8).

example, do you hold a child in elementary school accountable for not knowing Einstein's equations, and beat him? It is the same with God and His teachings. He holds us accountable for teachings that we are able to grasp, in accordance with our Preserved Tablet. We should not let the teachings consume us. Rather we should try to reach true peace while we are in this world. Peace means being in the presence of God. A person who is in the presence of God is at peace in each moment. No one can affect his peace. A person who finds peace in the presence of God will pity the tyrant because he knows what the outcome will be.

An oppressed person, who will attain true peace by the grace of God, pities his oppressors. Let's explain this further: a man went to his shaykh. Referring to a corrupt group of people, he said, "O master! These people are openly violating the divine laws. Curse them so that they start to live according to God's decree, so that they are punished and understand that what they are doing is wrong!" On hearing this, the shaykh opened his palms in supplication and said: "O Lord! These people seem to thoroughly enjoy what they do in this world. By your grace, grant them the same happiness and enjoyment in the Hereafter!" Dumbfounded, the disciple asked, "O master! I asked you to curse them, but you blessed them with your supplication!" This time the shaykh said, "My son! Could there possibly be a greater curse than this? They have so much fun in this world. If they continue on the same path, they will never find the way to heaven. In order for them to find heaven in the next world, they must be free from corruption. This process of purification entails a lot of pain. So there can be no greater curse for a human being than this!" Speaking of cursing, it is, God forbid, a terrible thing to do! It is tantamount to instructing God what to do. My late teacher Samiha Ayverdi used to tell us, "Cursing someone is similar to telling God, 'Hey, You don't know how to punish so and so; let me teach you how to do it!' It is a serious transgression and oversteps the bounds of servitude!" For this reason, friends and lovers of God refrain from cursing and tremble at the thought of doing anything against God's will. A friend of God was traveling across a certain land, when the following thought occurred to him: "O Lord, You shower abundant rain on this piece of land which is already fertile. Meanwhile, this other piece of land is utterly barren but You don't let a single drop of rain fall there. Is this just?" Not even a second later he began to shake violently, and with great remorse said, "What have I done? I tried to interfere with God's wisdom and justice. It is as if I uttered a curse!" In the hope of being redeemed of this grave error, he tied a rope around his neck and made a passerby drag him for kilometers. That was how he earned his forgiveness. Cursing is the most unbecoming, indecent way to interfere in God's business. May God protect us from it!

Q: How do we know whether we are observing *edep* while praying or making supplication?

A: There are two very important stages while praying. The first is to make a request, saying, "O God, please grant me this and that...." There is a danger at this stage. Mevlana Rumi says, "This is the path of poverty (*fakr*); here you are granted all your desires and anything that you might have wished for earlier. Whether you wish to defeat an army, to chase away an enemy, to capture territory, to imprison a people, or to be superior to your peers. All these wishes and those similar to it will be granted to you if you have chosen the path of poverty. Followers of the path of poverty do not complain. Meanwhile, from amongst the hundreds of thousands of people who follow other paths, only a few are granted what they wish, and that too not in an entirely satisfying way. For any desire to be satisfied, and for any wish to be granted, there are certain principles that must be observed. The granting of desires is contingent on those principles. This path is long and has many obstacles and hardships. It may be that the principles are not in harmony with the thing desired. But because you are on the path of poverty and are occupied with it, God grants you unimaginable worlds and riches. At this point you become terribly ashamed that you asked for such trivial and petty things earlier. But then God says to you, "You have indeed risen above such wants and desires; you are above the stage of asking for such things; you are tired and uninterested and no longer desire these things. At one time, the idea of possessing these things had come to you, but you renounced it all for Me. My generosity is infinite. Now, I will surely grant you those things as well."

The Prophet, before reaching the Truth and gaining the fame that he did, saw the eloquence and sophistication of the speech of Arabs and said: "I wish I had such eloquence and sophistication of speech!" But when the world of the Unseen was unveiled to him, he forgot himself in the presence of God, and this wish that he had once made was reduced to nothing. Then the Lord most Great said, "O Muhammad, I have granted you perfect eloquence and sophistication of speech." The Prophet said, "O Lord, what good is it to me now? I have moved away from this desire." To this, God replied, "Don't feel bad. It has been granted to you. You no longer need to renounce it." Then God gave him such a Book that thousands of volumes have been written on it ever since to try to understand it; exegetes continue to write commentaries on the Qur'an, but no one has been able to fully understand it.

When God is so fond of giving, why do you set limits for His generosity by asking for only one thing? For example, we pray that we be endowed with knowledge. This seems like a perfectly wonderful thing to ask for. But with this request we have already set a limit. If we refrain from setting limits in prayer, He might grant us health, love, and true humility in addition to knowledge! We separated knowledge from a whole string of needs and asked for nothing else. Moreover, we can never be certain that the knowledge we have prayed for won't make us arrogant and self-righteous, because we don't know the station of our *nefis*. So with this supplication, we ask for something from God, the real value of which – in relation to our current state – we remain unaware. A real gnostic (*arif bi'Llah*) would say, "O God, give me what is good for me." This is the essence of prayer. Prayer is a means for strengthening the connection between God and humans. It is not simply wanting and asking things from God. At the same time, we know that He said, "Ask Me and I shall give, supplicate Me and I shall give." We are servants, so naturally we have needs and desires. If we ask in a way that reminds us of our servitude, then the true meaning of prayer will be evident. The best way to pray to God for something is to say, "O Lord, You know much better than I do what is good or bad for me." May God grant us all this contentment! It is such a virtue, such an important skill.

Speaking of the inner meaning of supplication, some requests are particularly pleasing to God, such as Zachariah's prayer for a child despite his old age. It should not be regarded as excessive or improper to say, "I want a child." God granted him a child despite his old age and despite the fact that his wife was barren. Mevlana Rumi says that God accepted Zachariah's prayer because of the unshakable faith and trust he had in God, and because he prayed for what seemed to be the most difficult of things, for what was considered to be impossible. The inner meaning of Zachariah's prayer is: "My *nefis* has fallen in love with my spirit. They have united, but my *nefis* is barren, and I am just too old. I have yet to produce the offspring of the heart (*veled-i kalb*; Ar. *walad al-qalb*). Let this meaning (that has come forth from me) be my posterity." So many prophets came from that spiritual lineage. There are many such supplications that lead to beautiful outcomes. May God grant us such supplications!

Q: I wonder what type of path should be followed for training the *nefis*?

A: I am a humble, simple teacher. But I have seen that love and kindness are very successful tools for any kind of teaching. I have seen that God blessed us with this through the Qur'anic verses. He told Moses "to speak softly to Pharaoh" so that Pharaoh could accept his message; so, teaching through kindness is a good method. When Ahmad al-Rifa'i (d. 578/1182) would address the people who were at the "station of teaching" (*Rabb maqam*; Ar. *maqam al-Rabb*), he would tell them that they should incline towards kindness because love and kindness are the only paths that take a human being to God. In our own training as well, the goal is not to get rid of all desires of the ego in one instant. My late Qur'an teacher, Hayri Bilecik, used to say, "Do not shut the main valves; rather, cut the smaller pipes so you can easily control the water flow." What does this mean? Do not deny the *nefis* its excessive desires all at once. Start with the smaller ones. Ask yourself, for example, what is the easiest action to take? Is it to stop lying? Good. Stop lying first. The point is that renouncing what seem to be minor faults of the *nefis* might lead to greater outcomes. Don't underestimate the minor faults. That is what he would say. So, a person should be gentle with his *nefis*, recognizing that the body is made from clay. A person should remain aware that God's majesty has a major effect on the body, causing it to quiver and quake. Of course, hardship will afflict the body. But to react by blaming ourselves and saying, "Why did I get so upset over nothing when I have been on this path for so many years?" comes only from the *nefis*. In the seventy-first verse of the chapter of the Cow (sura *al-Baqara*), Moses tells his people that the cow that is to be slaughtered must be one that is "not limited by the rules or customs of prescribed law (*şeriat*), not dwelling on itself, and not negatively inclined." [30] The cow in this verse is the *nefis*.

Q: Sufis say that the reality of *tevhid* is silence. Does silence mean to hold the tongue?

A: The reality of *tevhid* is silence; yes. Holding the tongue is best, but Ibn 'Arabi says that "asking to understand, to be certain, and to have a clear idea is very beneficial." The first step of holding the tongue is to stop objecting to the troubles with which you are afflicted. The second step is to be fully content in your heart. One day the Prophet was sitting with Abu Bakr. A man interrupted them and began to hurl abuses at Abu Bakr. When the Prophet saw that Abu Bakr was keeping quiet, he smiled. But when the man continued in an intolerable manner, Abu Bakr spoke up and defended himself, at which point the Prophet took his leave from there. Seeing this, Abu Bakr was saddened. He followed him and asked, "Why are you depriving me of your presence?" The Prophet answered: "When you kept quiet, an angel descended. When you began to defend yourself, a devil came. A prophet cannot be in the same place as devils."

Silence then, is of two types: silence of the tongue and silence of the heart. Silence of the tongue is to renounce all the idle talk and gossip that occupies us. To achieve this, we must ask ourselves each night, "How many times did I talk to God today?" Reflecting on and weighing the deeds of each day is very important. Benjamin Franklin is said to have called himself to account at the end of each day. He would ask, "What did I do today?" On one such day he concluded that he had done nothing wrong that day and went to sleep. After a while, he began to feel very uneasy, got up, and said to himself, "the worst thing I probably ever did was to decide that I did nothing wrong today." A human being is a servant of God; he makes mistakes. Wasting time on idle talk is torture for the human spirit.

The second type of silence, silence of the heart, is the station of "praise" (*hamd*). It is such a sublime station. The station of praise is higher than that of thankfulness (*şükür*; Ar. *shukr*). We are at the station of thankfulness when we express contentment with our tongues and our dispositions, for all the blessings that

---

30. "He replied, 'It is a perfect and unblemished cow, not trained to till the earth or water the fields.' They said, 'Now you have brought the truth,' and so they slaughtered it, though they almost failed to do so." Qur'an, *al-Baqara* (the Cow), (2:71). Tr. Haleem, *Qur'an*, p. 10.

God has granted. But to be at the station of praise means to express contentment in the face of trouble, affliction, and everything else. This is why it is such a sublime station.

> Q: Mevlana Rumi says in his *Fihi Ma Fihi*, "gratitude is a net that captures divine rewards. When the sound of gratitude reaches you, prepare to receive more. God afflicts the servants He loves. If they show patience, He chooses them for Himself. If they are grateful (for the affliction), He elects them. Some are grateful for His affliction and some for His graciousness. Both are good, for gratitude is the antidote for all occasions, changing wrath into grace."

A: This is why the station of praise is such a sublime state. When Abraham was cast into the fire, Gabriel came and asked him whether he had any wishes. He said, "When I have a wish, I ask God, not you." Gabriel replied, "Then ask from your Lord," to which Abraham replied, "Doesn't my God know me? About which need do I have to tell Him?"

When God loves a servant of His, He first sends him affliction. Being subjected to affliction is actually a great blessing for the human being. This is because in reality, the real affliction is the affliction of not knowing Who has sent the affliction! It is not unlike when someone is fixated on a piece of work and doesn't see who produced it. It is to cling to the rays of the sun. There is a beautiful story about this. It's an Indian story. A craftsman had an apprentice who worked for him. The apprentice was a real complainer; forget when he was faced with actual challenges – he even found something to complain about in all the blessings he possessed. When people complain this much, they begin to feel a tightness inside. They feel constricted. The craftsman, disturbed by the constant complaining of the apprentice, asked him to fetch a glass of water and put two spoons full of salt in it. Next he told the apprentice to drink it. On taking a sip, the apprentice spat it out, exclaiming, "O master, it tastes awful!" "Stop grumbling!" the craftsman said, "and bring another two spoons of salt." The man did as he was told. The craftsman led the apprentice to a lake with sweet water. "Now, throw the salt here," he said, and then instructed the apprentice to drink a glassful. The apprentice drank the water and remarked that it tasted quite good. The craftsman said, "O son, you have allowed your heart to become extremely small, as small as that glass, such that you need to spit out what you drink even when a little bit of salt enters it. You have lost all patience. If you stop complaining and find ways to be content with everything, the place of your heart will expand and challenges will not feel like challenges. Everything will be a blessing for you." So, we should give up our complaining altogether. Who are we going to complain about anyway? God?

Q: The purpose of affliction is to purify us. If we look at it this way, we can receive it well, right?

A: *Fitne* (Ar. *fitna*) (discriminatory test, temptation) is the greatest affliction. Do you know what it means? It is "fire that cleanses gold of copper." So when the challenge of *fitne* spreads, it distinguishes the gold-hearted from the copper-hearted. Consequently, all kinds of affliction bring out our inner beauties. In his discussion on the difference between the diamond and the coal, Muhammad Iqbal narrates the following: "Inside a coalmine, the coal said to the diamond: 'O you who has been blessed with eternity! We are friends, and whatever we have is the same.' (As you know, both coal and diamond are essentially pure carbon. Their components are exactly the same.) 'O you who has been blessed with eternity!' That is, O you who will not become extinct. 'We are friends. The essence of our existence in the world is the same. But I have no value; I keep melting away from my ore. But you! You adorn the crowns of sultans. I don't even have the value of earth. My nature is bad. While you cause the hearts of mirrors to shatter from envy, people watch me burn. They ought to weep on account of my condition. I am only a sparkle, while stars and beauty shine on your face and tongue!' The diamond replied: 'O thoughtful friend who can discern subtleties! It is only when the black earth bakes and is fully matured that it becomes jewelry to adorn rings. Diamonds must suffer tremendously, while coal is formed on the earth without any pain. This is why it is pitch black. Meanwhile, the diamond burns and burns underground for years on end through unbearable pressures and fires. Only after this much suffering does it transform into a diamond and become immortal. You burn because your body is soft, and because you cannot endure pain. Don't fear, don't suffer from sorrow, and don't be deceived.' To recap, the diamond tells coal, which has never endured any pain, not to fear, nor to be anxious or full of sorrow. From this we see that there are three ways of achieving maturity in this world: by not being fearful, sorrowful, and anxious. Be like a stone; be like a diamond. An industrious person who confronts hardship illuminates both worlds. Helplessness and worthlessness come from being uncooked and immature."

Q: Can we turn to the idea of "confidence or trust?" Specifically, when unpleasant things happen, is it possible for us to ever conclusively say, "Yes, I'm sure that this is from my God Who would never have given me anything bad. It is coming to me from Him in order to teach me."

A: What you just stated is the outlook of a confident individual. But since all of us are not at that level, and since we can't foresee how things will end up in the future, we are afraid. If only we knew that God has said, "the love a mother has for her child is a mere bubble compared to My love for you." One of His beautiful names is "the Lord of Majesty and Bounty." There is bounty hidden beneath His majesty. There is blessing after affliction. We should remember that Mevlana Rumi's name is Jalal al-Din (Majesty of Religion). The *Mathnawi* and *Fihi Ma Fihi*, among the greatest books of all times, came from the name of majesty. If this is true – and it certainly is – how beautiful are the heights to which the person who shows patience during pain will be taken!

Q: In *Fihi Ma Fihi*, Mevlana Rumi states: "Someone said to Muhammad, 'I love you,' to which the Prophet replied, 'Gather your senses, do you know what you are saying?' He repeated that he loved the Prophet. The Prophet then said, 'In that case be persistent in this because I will kill you with my own hands, poor you!'"

A: Yes, this refers to one of the Prophet's teaching methods. The statement, "I will kill you," means: "I won't let go of you until I completely purge you of the love you have for your life, property, children, and everything that you worship. I will challenge you with misfortune and affliction." The claim that one loves the Beloved of God – the pure manifestation of God's Essence – has to be demonstrated. The Prophet says, "I won't let go of you unless I cleanse you of your inclination to associate partners with God." I want to connect this to our topic of *edep*; I will explain *edep* through a story about 'Ali. It was Ramadan (the month of fasting), and the weather was scorching hot. The Prophet called out to one of his companions and said, "Slice this watermelon." The companion said, "O Messenger of God, with your permission, let me hang this watermelon in a cold well. You are fasting now; if I slice it, it will go bad by sundown. Please, let me slice it near dusk so I can treat you to slices of cold, refreshing watermelon." He asked another companion and got the same response. He then called 'Ali and said "'Ali, cut this watermelon." Without hesitating for even a second, 'Ali cut the watermelon. The other two companions objected and said, "O 'Ali, we could have cut it too, but there is still a long time left before sundown. That's why we didn't cut it." 'Ali replied, "It is he who taught me to fast and the times between which to fast. I do not rely on my reason when it is he who says this. I have sacrificed my reason for him. I regard all his wishes as *edep*, because he is the manifestation of the Truth." On hearing this, the Prophet said, "There is nobody who knows 'Ali save God and myself. There is nobody who knows me save God and 'Ali. And there is nobody who knows God save myself and 'Ali." This is the real meaning of *edep*.

Q: You are of course familiar with the story from the *Mathnawi*, in which Adam blames himself while Satan says to God, "You led me astray." Satan's act has been deemed as inappropriate (without *edep*), while Adam's act has been celebrated for exemplifying *edep*. Could you please explain this difference for us?

A: *Edep* is to reach the stations of the Unity of Attributes (*tevhid-i sifat*; Ar. *sifat al-tawhidi*) and the Unity of the Essence (*tevhid-i zat*; Ar. *dhat al-tawhidi*) and not to settle for the station of the Unity of Actions (*tevhid-i ef'al*; Ar. *af'al al-tawhidi*). Let me first explain the meaning of these stations. Unity of Actions is the station of witnessing God in every place and action. The highest level of this state is that of Satan because Satan reached the level of seeing God in actions. But if we settle for this station, rather if we get stuck here, we can't ascend to seeing God in the Attributes and the Essence.

Q: Is Satan the possessor of the name Deviation (*zal*; Ar. *dal*), and is Satan the one who manifests the actions of the name Deviation?

A: As possessor of the name "deviation," Satan was at the level of Unity of Actions, and failed to see the attributes and the essence.

He couldn't perceive the light of the manifestation of Truth in Adam, who had been created from clay.

God says, "I have created Adam in the form of the Merciful."[31] One of the meanings of "I have created in My own image" is "I have created in the form of the name of Muhammad." Even the Arabic letters that form this blessed name are the image of the human being. The M (م) is the head, the H (ح) is the body, the second M (م) is the abdomen, and the D (د) is the legs. The form of the human was created in the form of Muhammad's name. The meaning of Muhammad is "the most near." The human being is most near to God. Thus, God's statement has the implicit meaning of, "I manifest Myself from him." Unfortunately, Satan couldn't see this manifestation in Adam. Farid al-Din 'Attar said, "Satan did sense that divine essence in Adam, but he was in love with God. He couldn't accept sharing Him." Satan said, "He is mine alone." When God addressed all the angels and said, "Prostrate before Adam," some immediately obeyed and prostrated themselves. This is the meaning of the first prostration in prayer. When they raised their heads from the first prostration, they saw God's light in Adam, and prostrated for a second time without being ordered to do so. This is the meaning of the second prostration in prayer. But one group from among the angels never prostrated; they were the satans.

Some of them performed the first prostration, but did not repeat it because they couldn't see the light (in Adam). These represent the people of the husk; they remain at the form of prescribed law (Şeriat) and cannot reach its meaning. There is a third group among them; initially, they did not obey the divine command and did not perform the first prostration, but through God's grace, they saw the light and performed the second prostration. These represent people who reached God's meaning. The friends and lovers of God (evliya; Ar. awliya) are the ones who performed both prostrations. After this last group performed prostrations, Satan said, "Why should I prostrate myself when I was created from fire and Adam was created from clay?" Actually, Adam's clay was from light. He failed to see this. He also failed to recognize the universal intellect (külli akl), which was also Adam's light. Even though Adam contained all the names and attributes of God, Satan couldn't see this and disobeyed the command. Instead, he said, "I

---

31. *Al-Rahman* or the Merciful is one of the ninety-nine names of God.

am right;" it was Iblis who said "I," and "I am superior."

There is a parable about this. One day, 'Umar[32] took hold of Satan and said, "I am going to dishonor you and make a fool of you in front of everyone!" Satan replied, "After teaching all the angels for a thousand years, I only said 'I' once and fell. You were an idol-worshipper until only a few years ago; you buried your daughters alive. Aren't you ashamed of your past state?" 'Umar started crying and let him go, saying, "O Satan, you are right!" Satan is such a helpless, wretched being. In fact, it was Iblis, because it was Iblis' fate to say "I." When God extended His hand, Satan kissed His feet. "This is bad luck," Mevlana Rumi remarks – this is metaphorical, so please don't take it literally. Adam, on the other hand, is a great sultan. He said, "There is no being save Yours. Both Satan and I have ended up like this because of Your predestined command. But I made a mistake and was cast out of paradise. I am the tiniest of particles. You are the whole. I cannot place the blame of a particle on the whole; I condemn such improper behavior." Adam's *edep* was received very well by God and he was made a prophet. "Adam" actually means Perfected Human. Today, there are still Perfected Humans who convey Adam's meaning and God's names and attributes. They don't gloat or promote themselves, they don't brag. They are people of *edep*. Mevlana Rumi has pointed out, "But those who don't accept that they (Perfected Humans) are greater and different from them are at the station of Satan."

A friend of God has the power to turn the dirty blood of a gazelle into musk. The ability to turn dirty blood into musk is the secret of a pouch located in the abdomen of a gazelle. The elixir that transforms copper into gold is also hidden in the hearts (of God's friends). The blood that is in the heart becomes egotism, ambition, and avarice in you, while in them it becomes divine light. Like bread on a table, and water that gives life to everything that exists, they become the source of faith, goodness, beauty, and health in the body. The same venerable piece of food that is bread becomes contemptible, despicable, and dirty in a body given to the inclinations of the *nefis,* which is like a body that is no longer living. Yet the same bread becomes food for greatness, beauty, and goodness in the bodies of saints.

In her book, titled *Wayfarer: Where are you going?* my late teacher

32. See Glossary.

Samiha Ayverdi explained what Satan is.[33] She asked, "Why do you continue to get angry with Satan? Satan is nothing but a mirror. If you are ugly, he reflects your ugliness, and if you are beautiful, he reflects your beauty. Eventually, he will turn to you and insist: 'All I did was to say "You'd better do it this way," nothing more; why did you choose to obey me?' What this means is that Satan makes the ugliness that is part of us apparent. This was the level of Adam's *edep*, then it developed and matured, ultimately reaching the station of Muhammadan *edep*. Adam confessed, 'I can't place the blame of a single particle on the whole.' But the *edep* of the Prophet Muhammad was so excellent that in sura *al-Najm*, God says: 'God swears on the declining star.' That star is the Prophet. He ascended and returned. He didn't exceed his limits, nor was he puzzled."[34]

Q: What is the wisdom behind the Prophet's demand to come to this world as a "servant" prophet?

A: The Truth will manifest in you in direct proportion to your success at humbling yourself in servitude, and in achieving self-negation and nothingness. If we have even an atom's worth of existence (*varlık*) in us, the truth cannot manifest in us. Let me respond to your question with a story from the *Mathnawi*. One day, a competition was organized between the Turks and Mongols. They were each to paint opposite facing walls that were separated by a curtain in between. The Mongols produced a truly magnificent piece, an exceedingly beautiful picture with a brilliant color configuration. Meanwhile the Turks were persistently carving, sandpapering, and polishing the wall such that no "I-ness" would remain. Eventually, all coarseness was removed from the wall; it had become "a perfect servant." The curtain was then pulled aside. No doubt, the wall painted by the Mongols was breathtaking; it distributed the beauty and majesty of God in the most perfect colors. As for the opposite facing wall, it had become an impeccably polished mirror that displayed a sparkling reflection of the Mongol painting. And it was declared the winner of the competition due to the sheer intensity of the manifestation that it reflected. Just like this, when God's beauty reflected on the polished mirror of the servant Prophet, a masterpiece came into being. The Prophet was this masterpiece.

---

33. Samiha Ayverdi, *Yolcu, Nereye Gidiyorsun? (Wayfarer: Where are you going?)*, (Istanbul: Kubbealti Neşriyati, 1975), 3rd edition, page 153-154.

34. Qur'an, sura *al-Najm* (the Star) (53:1).

Q: In light of what you have just discussed, is it correct to say that the real meaning of *edep* is servitude? The Prophet occupied the highest level of servitude during the ascension (*mirac*).

A: *Edep* means to attribute no being whatsoever to yourself and to see no existence in yourself. This is to say that the goal of all the paths leading to God is *edep*. All Sufis have said, "*Edep* is a crown of divine light. Once it rests over your head, go wherever you wish to go." Those without *edep* are losers in both worlds. In reality, all forms of wicked behavior like hypocrisy, arrogance, dishonesty, self-righteousness, and backbiting are rooted in our failure to be faithful servants of God and our inability to annihilate the "I" that lies between God and us. But if we are always with God, and if we see and know nothing but Him, then with whom could we be arrogant and about whom could we speak ill? All negative traits appear in the course of our interactions with people. When we are able to see the world beyond its temporal, created form, then we will no longer be envious, hypocritical, or arrogant. What I mean is, instead of saying or thinking, "Ahmed did this to me," or "Mehmet upset me very much," we should bring ourselves to say, "God subjected me to this for my own good. And for my sake, poor so and so, who was only the vehicle, had to carry out that duty." This is the meaning of true peace. Ultimately, it is crucial to realize that that which is created does not really exist. Severing the ties we have to all that is created allows the veils of "I" or "We" to be removed from our hearts. But we must feel, and indeed *live* this negation in our hearts.

We must continue to fulfill the duties and responsibilities incumbent on us as faithfully as possible. But we must remain aware that all our interactions and affiliations are not with other people; rather, they are encounters with God. We must understand this in order to earn God's contentment. Understanding this will bring us peace. Earlier, we said that being at peace is to be in the presence of God.[35] The goal of worship is peace and the goal of being in the presence of God is *edep*. This is to say that if worship brings us peace, then what we call worship is what allows us to reach the presence of God. *Edep* means to hurt no one and to be hurt by none. We also see that *edep* is the meaning of the Qur'an. My teacher used to say, "From all that is beautiful in this world,

---

35. The term "*hudur*" in Arabic and in Turkish means both peace and presence.

there are three things I love: love (*aşk*), *edep,* and mystical knowledge (*irfan*)." Without *edep,* love and mystical knowledge are not complete. Mystical knowledge is the ability to say and live "There is no god but God," that is, to unite the whole universe. It is to penetrate the secret of "Things appear to the knower as names / and in all the names the Namer appears."[36] The goal of *edep* is servitude. And the goal of servitude is to earn God's contentment (*rıza*).

If you were to ask, "how is it possible to earn God's contentment?" Well, we should learn from those who have earned it. Let me explain this through a story. There was a man, a very simple man, who would ask everyone what he needed to do to please his Lord. Someone advised him to find God's *rıza.*[37] He said, "Okay, I see. I need to find God's *rıza.*" Eventually he found a man named *Rıza* who happened to be a gnostic. *Rıza* said to the man, "Finding me is not enough to gain God's *rıza.* You have to do more to seek His pleasure. You have to worship Him." The man said to *Rıza* that he didn't know how to do anything more. "Make supplications," *Rıza* said. "By God, I don't even know how to pray," the man confessed. "Well, what is it that you know best?" *Rıza* asked. To this the man said, "The only thing I know is a village dance." "So do it! Do it for the sake of God," *Rıza* replied. The man complied and began to perform the dance for God. *Rıza* saw a crown of light descend from heaven and rest over the man's head. *Rıza* was taken aback, as he had never seen such a crown despite the many years he'd spent striving and being steadfast. He said, "you have danced beautifully for God, so beautifully that I saw a crown of light descend on your head!" The simple man replied, "Oh yes, it is all because I found *Rıza!*"

Our intention is what truly matters, not the form. Real worship is all that is done for the sake of God alone. If everything we do is for God, then we will eventually be led to His presence. For someone to meaningfully say: "There is no god but God," they must first demonstrate the beautiful names of God. Lovers of God have the best *edep* because every single thing they do is for God. Even behavior that appears to lack *edep* is in fact nothing but *edep.* Once, such a lover of God had grown some stubble and was wandering around teasing God, "O my beloved! You have given me no money,

---

36. Niyazi Mısri, *Niyazi Misri Divani Şerhi,* Ed. Seyyid Muhammed Nuru'l-Arabi, (Istanbul: H Publishing, 2014).

37. In Turkish (and other languages), "*Rıza*" is also the name for a male.

so I can't afford to go to a barber. And look at my stubble!" As soon as he uttered these words, the tree that stood before him turned into pure gold. "My beautiful King! One should know better than to joke with you!" The best *edep* is that of a lover of God because it is pure and comes straight from the heart.

As for the inner and outer meanings of *edep*, outer *edep* is to find God through worship. It is to attain peace (through worship). Inner *edep*, on the other hand, is to maintain the state where you are with God in your heart at all times, no matter what you might be doing outwardly. Perhaps another meaning of *edep* is to know our limits – as we see in the example of our Prophet – and to never transgress those limits. It is to be able to say, "O God, I have such and such qualities; help me to improve through these qualities." Let me put it another way: an ant was once making the journey towards Mecca for the Hajj pilgrimage. "You cannot make it," everyone said to it. The ant replied, "At least I am on my way."

In a similar story, when the prophet Joseph was for sale, the Egyptians wanted very much to purchase him. When the bidders grew in number, the sellers asked for musk five or ten times the weight of Joseph. Suddenly, an old woman with a few balls of yarn appeared in the middle of the crowd and announced: "O crier who is selling the Joseph of Kenan! My love for this child has swept me away. I have spun ten complete balls of yarn to purchase him. Take these balls of yarn and sell Joseph to me. Don't say a word just hand him to me." The seller scoffed and said, "You naïve woman, this gleaming pearl is not within your means. He is worth a treasure. What makes you think you can buy him with a few balls of yarn? " The old woman replied, "I know very well that no one can buy this boy with these balls of yarn. But it is enough for me that everybody here, be they an enemy or a friend, will be a witness to the fact that I was also a seeker of Joseph."

An enlightened heart (*gönül*) that is strong in its determination and active in its efforts will immediately attain eternal blessing.

According to another story, a man once said to Moses, "Please, Moses, ask God if He loves me." Moses did as he had been requested, and God replied with a question: "that servant of Mine?" Since there was nothing for Moses to tell the man, he remained silent. But the man was persistent. He asked, "O Moses, did He not say anything at all about me?" Finally, Moses said, "All He said was 'that servant of Mine?'" On hearing this, the man was overcome with joy. He understood his station, and said, "He has seen me fit to be a servant and referred to me as 'My servant'. Could I ask for a greater blessing?"

We have said that the meaning of *edep* is to establish a connection with God. Another meaning is to patiently wait until we are spiritually mature. The most important thing though is to embody servitude. The state of servitude compels us to cut every affiliation except our affiliation with the master. It is to renounce everything that is secondary (*cüzi*) or primary (*külli*). It is to be able to say, "I have cleansed my heart of everything except my God. Outwardly I care about my appearance and dress neatly so that I look decent to people while serving my God. But in my heart and in the core of my being I do everything for Him alone."

To embody servitude means to renounce all desire for honor and rank (which is a blessing). What kind of honor and blessing are to be renounced? A friend of God (*veli*) was to be hung. Why would a friend of God be hung? Because that was how much he desired death. He begged Shams of Tabriz, "O Shams, please pray to God that I be reunited with Him." Shams offered a supplication and it was accepted. The man was slandered and caught, and was awaiting execution. Shams went up to the man appointed to do the hanging and gently patted him. The people who had come to watch the execution were bewildered, "What kind of man is this? He is comforting the executioner!" they said. Later, Shams explained: "The man who was to be hung was a friend of God; executing him was not easy. But he wanted so much to die. What I did was to give the executioner strength." But that great teacher had touched his hand. Meanwhile just before being hung, the friend of God made the following prayer: "Oh God, You have granted me an elevated station in this world as among the friends of God. Please take this from me. I want to come to You as nothing, as a servant. I want to return as non-existent, as pure nothing. Give my station to this man, the executioner." Both these experiences, being touched by Shams and the immense difficulty of executing God's friend, elevated the executioner to the station of a saint. As for God's friend, he was reunited with His Lord as nothing. Could there be a greater blessing than this?

To be in a state of servitude means that you don't assign a superior place to your *nefis,* nor do you privilege yourself over other people. In fact, to be a servant of God means to walk out on the street and see that everybody else is superior to you – at least in some respect. To be a servant of God is to know your limits as a human being. It is to always be in awe of God and to submit to His Will. A servant of God cannot become a Perfected Human until he is no longer enslaved to others and the desire to please others. The following saying of Diogenes to Alexander establishes that he was a Perfected Human: "You are a slave to my slave (that is, you are a slave to your *nefis* which, in me, has been subdued to my will). Why should I, a completely free man, salute a person who has made himself a slave?"

> Q: There is still one thing that I am unclear on, and I would appreciate it if you could say more about it. How can we reach a state where we don't see ourselves as superior to others? It is not easy to regard every passer-by in the street as superior to us.

A: There is some truth to this. But every person in the street has their own profession and we lack the abilities that they have with respect to that profession. We can't cook as well as a chef, can we? Or if we see a donkey on the street, we are incapable of carrying even half the load that it can carry. All our abilities have a limit. How then do we presume to have any power?

I have mentioned this several times: a film was showing in the theaters last year called "Iris." I wish everyone could see it; it teaches us a very important lesson. It is about one of the most famous female authors in England. She is seventy years old but still participates at conferences; on many occasions she has to decline invitations on account of her busy schedule. Her novels are bestsellers the moment they hit the shelves. She completely over-shadows her husband. Then, all of a sudden, she is afflicted with Alzheimer's disease and loses everything. She goes from being a vibrant woman with a great intellect to a woman who spends her time playing with her feces.

So really, about which fleeting quality of ours can we feel good and gloat to others? Our intellect? Our ideas? Our temporary beauty that will inevitably leave us? A person younger than us, even by one year, has fresher skin. Someone two years younger has better vision. As we move further into old age, our ears and body gradually lose function and we lose our hair. Our wealth and property will also soon leave us. Or let's assume it stays. How much of it can we take with us to our grave? So let's think: which of our qualities or abilities can we boast about given that they are all transient and will soon be taken away from us? Even the love we have for God and the service we do with love doesn't have significance. These are essential blessings (*zati ikram;* Ar. *al-ikram al-dhati*) of God that have been granted to us. What is an essential blessing? It is when He grants us something without expecting anything in return and makes us treat others the same way, thereby teaching us the pleasure of giving away without expecting anything in return. This is an essential blessing. The essential blessings given by God are our "capital" in the Hereafter and nothing else.

Q: While speaking about the *mirac* (ascension) just now, you said that all of us are capable of making this ascension. How is it possible for us to achieve this?

A: It is possible because our master the Prophet said so. And if it is he who said it, it is true. Our *mirac* cannot be like that of the Prophet Muhammad. He is the king of kings. Each person's *mirac* is based on his or her capacity. It is said that prayer is *mirac*. Those who have understood the inner meanings of worship, and who worship only for God, and those who have thus reached the station of witnessing God in each person and thing, are actually experiencing their *mirac*. This is how the Prophet also explains it. Kenan Rifa'i also says that what is meant by *mirac* is to find God. God doesn't give this to everybody; people experience their *mirac* in varying degrees but always according to their capacities. Even if a person forgives one thing, in that act of forgiving is the realization of God's manifestation. It is a great blessing to realize God's manifestation. May God make us worthy of this blessing! Being aware of our state as servants of God is of utmost importance for *mirac*. It is the state of servitude that takes a person on their *mirac*. Similarly, *edep* takes a person on their *mirac*. May God never allow these to be missing in our lives! Ahmed Rifa'i says, "O righteous one! Don't fall prey to the problems of self-importance and self-righteousness. Don't be arrogant." Such qualities lead to a person's own destruction because those who despise others while thinking of themselves as superior cannot find God.

Each one of us is a helpless being. Our origin is a drop of stinky water and eventually, we will end up as stinky carrions. There is no doubt that what endows the human body with honor is the jewel of intellect. The essence of intellect is that it takes hold of the *nefis* and ties it extremely tightly. There is a saying of Ahmed Rifa'i that the human body consists of a spirit and a *nefis,* which are equipped with the quality of Lordship. The only thing that can serve as a link between these two is the intellect. But the intellect needs illumination. Without light, it cannot see; it is created and works according to the principle of opposites. And this light is a divine light that manifests in the heart through the guidance of teachers. When this light hits the heart, it is called an illuminated heart and it begins to illuminate the intellect. The intellect is disturbed by the terrible actions of the *nefis,* and begins to warn the *nefis.* After receiving warning from the intellect, the *nefis* starts to sense its own truth and nothingness. It thinks to itself, "all this time I have been nothing, non-existent, and I will be nothing; the intellect is teaching me this." It searches the body for something stronger, more formidable, and more meaningful than itself. It discovers the spirit and fulfills the Prophet's saying, "He who knows himself knows his Lord." He who knows himself, that is, he who comes to realize his essential non-existence and discovers the spirit that holds the station of lordship, not only *discovers* the spirit, but slowly becomes a lover. Once the *nefis* becomes a lover, it wants to be annihilated in the thing that it loves and it is annihilated in the spirit. "That which was first named *nefis* became the spirit; how praiseworthy!" With this manifestation (*tecelli;* Ar. *tajalli*), that is, by maturing, it joined the spirit. Actually, the *nefis* doesn't die, it becomes one with the spirit. This is the station of Joseph, and can also be called the station of the Perfected Human. All this depends on our ability to perceive our essential nothingness and non-existence. If the intellect doesn't control the *nefis,* it can't be called "intellect." It is only when it controls the excessive desires of the *nefis* that it has any worth.

When a person is deprived of this essence of intellect, their body is nothing but hollow physical matter, lacking in any meaning. It has no value at all. But if the intellect attains perfection, Mevlana Rumi says, "its owner becomes the crown of kings, thanks to this treasure." The stations of the intellect must save the person from lying and selfishness. Mevlana Rumi says that when the intellect prevails its owner stops dictating everything. He stops saying, "I know everything, I can do everything, and I have learned everything!" He begins to rely completely on God, to think deeply and say, "I hope to do this with God's help and blessing. I pray He gives me the strength to do it." Once he is adorned with the jewel of intellect, that intellect occupies the highest place in that person. Nevertheless, human beings must never abandon humility; they should continue to think about their origin and ultimate destination. They must show moderation and balance in everything they do. They should choose their words and actions accordingly. Divine counsel is ever present in the heart of every believer. No one and nothing can benefit a person who is not a good counsel for him/ herself. A wretched person whose heart is covered with the veils of heedlessness does not benefit from advice given by anyone.

Here, Mevlana Rumi says, "Everything existed in us in pre-eternity; in this life we simply remember what we had in pre-eternity." And if, as we remember this, we don't offer ourselves good counsel, no advice coming from outside will ever benefit us. Of course, when we go to a doctor, even if it is in order to quit a selfish addiction like smoking, the first question the doctor asks us is, "Have you made this decision yourself?" Similarly, a spiritual guide will ask the same question, "Have you resolved to struggle against your *nefis*?" Of course, if the individual sits in front of the teacher, the guide will facilitate the process through the teaching of love. But ultimately it is up to us to take the decision. So the most effective medication for a person lies within him or herself. "When you speak, speak words of benevolence," my teacher says. When you do something, do it right and do what is comfortable; that is, do what is pleasing to God. Be a friend only to good people and keep company with good people.

Remember what God says: "When two people are speaking of Me fondly, I am there as a third." In every state, be it during worship or otherwise, make sure you are clean and pure – both physically and spiritually. Don't worship God with only one part of the religion. Worship your God with sincerity and enthusiasm. Don't associate partners with Him. Let the path on which you walk be adorned by the words of your prophet, who is more favorable to you than your own self. When faced with difficulty, reach out for God's hand, seek help only from Him, and put your hopes only in Him. Welcome with patience what your Lord decrees for you. Never ever despair of His mercy, because it is only unbelievers who despair of His mercy. If you have a sound mind and if you are endowed with wisdom, it is only natural for you to place everything on the scales of wisdom and weigh them up that way. Whichever side weighs heavier, God will consider it weightier, and vice versa. In both situations, your decision will be based on *edep*. The veil between God and His creation will never be torn.

Such people always speak the Truth. On the path of God, they are not in the least bit afraid of being scorned by the despisers, and they are not ashamed in front of them. "O you brother!" Rumi says, "Be like this wise and honorable person. If your *nefis* transgresses its limits on account of being overcome by anxieties, or if it leans toward hubris and immoderate behavior, or if it makes you a tyrant out of envy, then seek refuge in God against this Satan. And remember God, and remember death through His remembrance. Death is the door of the path that leads to God. It is the door of the return to His absolute will. Death is the door to standing in the presence of God. At that door, remember the questions that He will ask you concerning everything. Don't forget the content of the secret of God's speech. There is no doubt that God constantly watches over us. Let us traverse the spiritual stations with our heart. Let us do things and own things that are clean and in compliance with the *Şeriat* and the intellect. Let us forsake things that are not in compliance and hence a source of doubt. Let our actions be pure – in order to ascend to the holy presence of God Who is above every kind of fault, conceivable, and inconceivable.

Beautiful words ascend only to Him.[38] They ascend through good deeds and actions. This is the meaning of *mirac*. The good word refers to beautiful people because God calls perfect humans "the Words of God." You remember the verse that begins with, "If all the trees on earth were pens and all the seas, with seven more seas besides, [were ink,] still God's words would not run out: God is almighty and all wise"?[39] If the qualities of such perfect, sublime people were to be written down, all the seas would run dry and all the trees would be exhausted. Just like that, such individuals are always ascending, always experiencing an uninterrupted state of *mirac*. God's words are divine verses. So "Perfected Human being" means divine revelatory verse. A divine revelatory verse is a miracle. This being the case, the Perfected Human is also a miracle of

---

38. This is a reference to Qur'an *al-Fatir* (the Creator), (35:10): "If anyone desires power, all power belongs to God; good words rise up to Him and He lifts up the righteous deed, but a severe torment awaits those who plot evil and their plotting will come to nothing." (Tr. Haleem, *Qur'an*, p. 277).

39. Qur'an, *Luqman*, (31:27). Tr. Haleem, *Qur'an*, p. 262.

God. The only reason the world has been created is for God to manifest Himself through such beautiful human beings. What a great blessing it is to understand and see this truth. When this truth is understood, the Qur'an removes the veil from its face and provides all kinds of treasures from its meaning. Rumi says, for the person who finds it difficult to be complete, that is, who doesn't succeed in uniting majesty and beauty, the Qur'an is veiled and very difficult to understand.

Q: I wonder if it is the same to say that the Qur'an doesn't remove its veil unless we present it with the "*yuzgorumlugu.*"[40]

A: Quite right. This "price" refers to the crushing of our egotistical desires, to attaining complete understanding of our state of servitude and nothingness, and to being ever aware of our essential non-existence. If we read the Qur'an after this offering, that is, if we read it as a servant of God, then we sense its infinite meaning and we don't try to impose limitations on it, in the same way that a Perfected Human being is limitless. The Prophet says, "The Perfected Human being and the Qur'an are twins." When the Qur'an is read this way, it is impossible to think, "All right, I have understood this and know it well enough." Instead, the Qur'an radiates infinite bezels of wisdom at each moment. We must always consider that every verse has "two hands." To put it simply, every verse has a *celali* (pertaining to Majesty) and *cemali* (pertaining to Beauty) interpretation. When we read the Qur'an we must do so with sincerity and by first removing our own selves, in the same way that we sit when we are in the presence of a Perfected Human being, by repressing our *nefis* and I-ness. This is what *edep* is all about.

---

40. A Turkish custom where, after the wedding, the groom would offer a present to the bride in exchange for permission to see her face by removing her veil.

Chapter Three:
Divine Decree and Destiny *(Kaza ve Kader)*

Q: The topic this evening is divine decree (*kaza*) and destiny (*kader*). Most people don't fully explain these terms. I'm hoping you might describe them to us in a way that we can understand.

A: I hope I can speak about it in a way that I can understand as well! This is one of the most challenging topics. It is hard to explain because it is understood differently, depending on one's level of understanding. God-willing, it will be explained and understood correctly this time. I want to begin our discussion with a poem by my teacher Kenan Rifa'i, in which he presents his view of destiny, and emphasizes that God predetermines all things. Here is the poem:

> Why all the effort, why the ambition?
> When there's no undoing the pre-eternal decision
>
> It is impossible to catch the bird of bliss in this world!
> Has a dream ever been caught by toiling undeterred?
>
> Said the beloved of God: "There is no comfort in the world"
> Anything you say to this will be futile and absurd
>
> One by one all who came have also gone away
> Does time allow anyone to escape from this place?
>
> Say not: "since I arrived, I have seen hardship at every turn"
> A day will come when for this very moment you will yearn

Look at the past, and at God's prophets
See what the enemies did to God's beloved

Reflect on what befell the grandchildren of the Messenger
O God! A heart-wrenching event, what suffering, what horror!

Many innocent were soaked in blood that day
Crying for a drop of water, they left burning with thirst that day

Look at them to measure how your own self fares
Consider the distance that separates your resolve from theirs

Your definition of torture and torment
Is not more than a drop when poured in their ocean of pain

O Kenan! Embrace for your *nefis,* sorrow and grief,
This is earthly life; it comes to us, and then it leaves.

My teacher explains in this wonderful poem that the law (*hükm*) of pre-eternity is inevitable and will never change. Also, that it is impossible to search for happiness in relation to this world, or to seek happiness from worldly experience (*zevk;* Ar. *dhawq*). He refers to a tradition of the Prophet, "*La rahata fi'l-dunya* (There is no ease in this world)." Those who expect ease in the world cannot find it. He says only a fool strives for the pleasures of this world alone. All (worldly) things are transient; nothing is permanent here, so what is it that you dwell on? On what do you rest your hopes? Why do you cry over the things you encounter (in this world)? If you are not content with what has happened to you, God will immerse you in even greater suffering such that you will wish for what you had before. As an example, my teacher refers to the great adversity that afflicted the grandsons of the Prophet and points out that what we complain about is but a speck of dust compared to what they suffered. Then he turns to himself, and in doing so also reminds us of the meaning of his name.[1] He says, "O Kenan, accept all the sorrows and afflictions that weigh heavily on your *nefis*, because they call this world '*dunya*' and it will never change. Understanding this is the most beautiful form of destiny. If we perceive affliction through a worldly lens, it appears as pain and suffering. But through the lens of the world and what lies beyond we see the wisdom behind all that occurs."

---

1. The name Kenan carries the meaning of "one who knows" and also "the place that one longs to reach."

Q: So what is the wisdom behind things that happen to us? And why do we complain about them?

A: All the things that happen to us are connected to the pre-eternal decision (*ezel hükm;* Ar. *hukm al-azal*). Let me try to explain divine decree and destiny. Divine decree is the state of things as summarized in the Preserved Tablet. It refers to the unchanging qualities and beautiful things written in our Preserved Tablet. God records these in our book of deeds so that our essence can be revealed. This record never changes. In order for the pre-eternal decision to be realized in accordance with a person's aptitude and constitution, destiny is lived out. In other words, destiny is the way in which the pre-eternal decision that has been written in our Preserved Tablet is lived out according to our aptitude. So the things that happen to us are the materialization of divine decree, the pre-eternal decision.

Q: You talked about "ability" (*istidat;* Ar. *isti'dad*). For people who have the same name, does that name manifest differently in accordance with their individual ability and disposition?

A: Yes, exactly. For instance, if it is written in someone's Preserved Tablet that they will become a killer, this will never change, but the destiny of the killer depends on their ability. If their disposition is of beauty and they are blessed with God's beautiful names, then they will be a killer because they killed an enemy during war; they are not called murderers, rather, heroes. So the pre-eternal decision will be realized as divine decree, but because their destiny is in accordance with their disposition, they will have become heroes. While it was divinely decreed that they were to be killers, they lived as heroes. By contrast, if a person is of a negative disposition and kills for the pleasure of his *nefis*, then he will be called a murderer. You will note that while divine decree is fixed, its external expression varies according to the disposition of each individual. This is what it is all about.

Q: So our essence and destiny are inevitable and inescapable. But can we still say that we are free in our actions?

A: Yes. Muhammad Iqbal says, "God has left human beings free to choose between good and bad because He trusts them. Human freedom rests on His trust." It is this freedom that we call "*cüz'i irade"* (*lit.* limited free will, or partial agency).[2] In other words, we call the capacity to choose our actions according to our ability "free will." What did we say was the relationship between divine decree and destiny? The pre-eternal decision is the decree, and the realization of the decision is destiny. In other words, destiny is the living out of that decision. Let's try to understand this through the example of the Prophet Adam. In Adam's Preserved Tablet, it was decreed that he would be the site for the manifestation of God's essence and meaning. That is, when God created Adam, He wrote in his Preserved Tablet that He would manifest His meaning through him. But Adam's rebellion against God was also decreed for him. This is because for Adam to become a site of the disclosure of God's Essence (*zat tecelli*; Ar. *dhat tajalli*), he had to make a mistake. In order for God to manifest in him, he had to be nothing, so he had to make a mistake. Adam's material existence had to be nothing. God would not manifest Himself through Adam unless he became, in terms of his material being, nothing and non-existent. Let's look at how this plays out.

It was God's decree that He would manifest in Adam and that Adam would make a mistake. It was once Adam understood his nothingness after his mistake that God's decree of manifesting in Adam was carried out. The story of Adam is central for explaining divine decree and destiny. Adam came to understand his nothingness and non-existence precisely by making a mistake. How do we know this? Through the conversation where God commands Satan to prostrate before Adam, and Satan refuses, saying, "I won't prostrate before him, because he is nothing and is created from clay, whereas I am from fire, so I have an existence." God then turned to Adam and said:

> O Adam, why did you go astray? Wasn't it I who led you astray? Satan says: 'If You had wished, You would have made me prostrate before Adam. But because You didn't and because You made me say 'I won't prostate myself' O God, it is You who are to blame.' Whereas you, Adam, you say that it was you who made a mistake, and you shed tears over it. Don't you understand that it was My wish that you be led astray?

---

2. Unlike God's will (*külli irade*), which is absolute, the will of human beings (*cüz'i irade*) is limited to the extent that it is dependent on God.

Adam replied, "I am limited, O God! I am nothing! Even if You were to manifest from me, because of my limited existence You would manifest with error. I am the one who makes mistakes, whereas You are above all mistakes. I cannot attribute my mistakes to You." Then God made Adam a prophet because Adam was aware of his own agency. He endowed him with divine qualities.

Thus, it is through striving and individual agency that a person is able to know his nothingness before God. This causes God to manifest from that person. Two statements confirm this: the saying of the Prophet, "I am the best of servants," and the saying of Ibn 'Arabi, "God manifested His essence in only two prophets." These two prophets are the first and the last. Because Adam said, "I am nothing," God manifested Himself in him, and because the Prophet Muhammad said, "I am nothing," God manifested Himself in him.

Q: We say that it is impossible to escape our divine decree and destiny, which means that these are fixed and don't change. What is the purpose then of all the prophets and friends of God who teach and discipline humanity?

A: Indeed, it is not possible to escape our decree and destiny. But divine decree is realized according to our individual abilities, and prophets were sent to help us develop our individual abilities. So divine decree is fixed, but the form of that decree varies according to each person's individual ability. A person preordained to be a killer, for example, can emerge as a hero. But this possibility is still contingent on his capacity to kill in a manner or for a cause that is heroic. The possessor of advanced ability could kill, but would do so as a hero, and in a manner that was acceptable to God. The purpose of teachers is to help people *develop* their abilities, to *show* them their abilities, and to *reveal* their hidden abilities. Human beings need teachers to learn chemistry and physics. A teacher talks about the physics and chemistry of a student's being and their meaning, about their essence. The student says, "All right, I understand." What she understands is what she already knows. This is how the perfect spiritual guide (*al-murshid al-kamil*) operates. She reveals to her students their own internal beauty and abilities. She strives towards that goal. And if the students have negative capacities, she reveals those negative capacities as well. So we see that the most critical role in the realization of divine decree and destiny is that played by the perfect spiritual guide; in other words, the role played by prophets and their successors.

Q: Do they function as catalysts?

A: We call this function "catalyst" in chemistry. You're accustomed to using chemical terms because you have been working with me. During a reaction where two substances unite without entering the reaction, the catalyst is the substance that speeds up the reaction and ensures that it happens. Sometimes the spiritual guide joins in that reaction, and others times he follows from a distance and accelerates that reaction. He reveals the person's inner self so that they can advance by means of their own inner foundation. This is the meaning of perfect spiritual guide. In chemistry, we refer to the substance that fulfills this role as the catalyst. In Sufism, it is the beloved of God.

Q: For students to emerge from this reaction with a positive outcome, they must approach the teacher without any doubts or presuppositions, yes?

A: Yes. Let me share a very subtle point. I'd like to congratulate Mrs. Emine Işınsu for the book she has written on the life of Niyazi-i Mısri (d. 1105/1694) entitled *Bukağı*. I've been reading this book and I hope and pray that more works such as this one and on the lives of ʿAli and his descendants get written. Approaching the teacher with doubt is like going to your doctor with doubt. It is equivalent to not taking the drug that your doctor prescribed because you're not sure if it will help you or hurt you, which then leads to the deterioration of your condition. Approaching the path shown by the teacher with doubts brings more harm than benefit. The way to submit to God is to submit ourselves to those that are more perfect than us, because the Truth (*Hakk*) is the created (*halk*), and the created (*halk*) is the Truth (*Hakk*). There is nothing more to it.

Q: It is related in the Qur'an that Moses went to the spot where the two seas meet and met Khidr there.[3] How did Khidr benefit Moses, given that Moses was already from among the greatest messengers?

---

3. See Glossary.

A: Yes, Moses was indeed one of the greatest messengers of God. Khidr, on the other hand, was the Perfected Human of that time when he came face to face with Moses. Moses said, "I," and also "I know." In the Chapter *Ta Ha,* God asks him, "What is that staff in your right hand, Moses?" He answers, "It is my intellect; I lean on it." Whatever we lean on in this world is our staff, like our intellect, self, or knowledge. Khidr can teach us the secret to abandoning these worldly and created things. God said, "Moses, throw down that staff." He threw it and the staff became a snake. What this shows is that the worldly things we rely on are created. These are things that God created and brought into existence through a process of change. They are bound to disappear.

Worldly things have been changed, and in order to reach wholeness they need to be corrected. This is why relying on them brings harm. A Perfected Human is needed to help us sever all ties with such artificial support. He teaches us to rely on the Creator (*Hakk*) and not on the created (*halk*). That is, he teaches us to rely on the heart, the meaning, the core, the essence, and the God in us, not on the intellect, self, body, beauty, knowledge, and everything that is acquired later in life. This is what Khidr did for Moses. It was after this that Moses became the master of two kinds of knowledge. He became "the place where the two seas meet." The same thing is related about Sadr al-Din Qunawi (d. 673/1274)[4], who is also called "a place where the two seas meet." "The meeting of the two seas" refers to the fact that these men of knowledge are masters of the knowledge of Şeriat (Normative Law) and the knowledge of *Hakikat* (Divine Reality). The way people understand the term Şeriat today is inaccurate. Şeriat means doing what is commanded to us by God for our benefit. What is the knowledge of Şeriat? It is the knowledge taught by God so that we may structure our lives and survive in this world. Seemingly non-religious disciplines like physics, chemistry, math, and biology are all included in the knowledge of Şeriat. What is the knowledge of *Hakikat*? It is the inner knowledge of these disciplines. Namely, the inner knowledge of physics is not the same as the knowledge of its apparent form. Rather, the inner knowledge of physics is concerned with reaching the meaning of God, which manifests in the apparent form of physics. Similarly, chemistry has to do with that which is within. What does the inner knowledge of

---

4. Sadr al-Din Qunawi was Ibn 'Arabi's most important disciple and the primary intermediary through whom his school gained influence.

chemistry mean? It is to find the life within the within. Knowledge is said to have found its destiny when it leads a person to God. The divine decree and destiny of that knowledge is to direct its recipient towards God. This brings us to a very important point. I suppose it was Muhiyyuddin Ibn 'Arabi who said, "Knowledge (*'ilm*) is hidden in that which is known (*ma'lum*). Knowledge belongs to God alone." Knowledge is for those among us who labor to learn. If a person doesn't internalize this knowledge, nor manifest it in her own personality, then what he has come to know cannot be claimed to have been properly learned.

If we don't simply store this knowledge in our heads, but rather know it well enough to apply it, and indeed become it, (and let me take it even further), if we use this knowledge in the right way such that it connects us with God, in other words, if we leave knowledge to its destiny, then what manifests from us will be true knowledge. And we will become true knowers. This is why true knowledge is destined to lead to God.

Let's return to the issue of divine decree and destiny. Adam was created so that when God would manifest through him, there would be light or essence from head to toe. Adam became the place that God's manifestation issued from, where the divine names and attributes were displayed. It was after this that God commanded all the angels to prostrate themselves before Adam. When the angels saw Adam blessed with divine manifestation, they prostrated before him as they did to God and they showed him respect because of his being blessed. What is the implied meaning here? It is the same as the meaning behind the two prostrations during prayer. Why are there two prostrations? The first is because God commanded it. God says, "I manifested in non-existence." This is God's understanding of decree and destiny. God manifests Himself in nothingness. What is nothingness? Earth! Earth is nothingness and is bound to become nothing. Earth represents nothingness. God sends His light to nothingness. God reflected His light on Adam who He created from earth. What happened as a result? He said to the angels, "Don't prostrate before Me; prostrate before the nothingness through which I manifest." There is great wisdom here. More than Himself, He orders prostration to those who see His meaning in His creation. What do I mean by this? He commands prostration to the Perfected Human, the Adam of the era. What does this mean? A person does not become a Muslim simply by proclaiming, "There is no god, but God." It is necessary to also say, "Muhammad is the messenger of God." Unless we prostrate before the Prophet, God's meaning cannot be understood. It is from this perspective that we can understand the command, "prostrate before Adam." The angels and some of the spirits prostrated themselves before Adam while others did not. After the prostration, some of the spirits held up their heads and saw, as is narrated in the Qur'an, the divine meaning and light on Adam's forehead, after which they did the second prostration in front of that light. Now, let's understand who constituted the different groups: namely, the group that made both prostrations, the group that only made the second prostration, and the group that didn't make the first or second prostration. The first prostration was obligatory. It is Şeriat. In fact, this command is the meaning of Şeriat. We are the ones who misunderstand the meaning of Şeriat.

If we use the term correctly, then Şeriat represents the things through which God commanded us to gain proximity to Him. All those who made the first prostration did so because they complied with Şeriat, or with the command (to achieve proximity to God). Among the followers of the Şeriat, some did not see the meaning, so they did not make the second prostration. They remained at the level of form. Those who performed both prostrations were the ones who observed the rules of the Şeriat and reached the meaning of Divine Truth. They saw that light, knew it, and made their prostration in awareness of it. In Sufism, we call this the level *hakikat* (Truth), and *marifet* (divine gnosis). Those who did not make the first prostration but made the second one upon seeing God's light in Adam are those special spirits on whom God bestows His mercy and shows His meaning despite their non-compliance with the Şeriat. They are so beautiful that I am reminded of something Mevlana said: "Make Qunawi lead the prayer. We are the substitutes (*abdal*) and don't know much about procedures, but Qunawi does. Praying behind him is like praying behind the Prophet." There are also those who did not make either of the prostrations. They are Satan and his cohort. Likewise, the spirits are also among such groups.

In this way, we can understand how Adam was blessed with God's manifestation. When Adam was a great vicegerent illuminating the meaning of God, and when he was taught all the divine names and qualities, why then did he commit an error and get sent to the world? Let's discuss this. The reason for Adam's lapse was that the knowledge that had been bestowed on him was not yet true knowledge, even though he was endowed with all the divine names. Let me explain. One of God's names is the Forgiver. We do not get to know this name until we realize the attribute corresponding to that name, in this case, forgiveness. So we do not know this name until we sin and are then forgiven by God for that sin. It is at this point that God manifests Himself with this name. We imagine God to have a name that corresponds to forgiveness, just like we imagine a word corresponding to the image of a Phoenix. However, for that name to be known to us, we must first commit a sin. Similarly, for us to know the name corresponding to love, the duality (of lover and beloved) is necessary. This is why Adam was sent to the world. How? God gave Eve to Adam as his wife but instructed them both, "Do not approach that tree, otherwise you will be among the transgressors." But could Adam and Eve have done anything else? The beautiful Lord had made that tree, the love tree, and just as He would speak to Moses from that same tree by saying, "I am your Lord," He spoke to them the same way. So they abandoned their intellect and approached the tree despite God's command to stay away from it. This is so because in the tree they saw God's manifestation.

Q: I'd like to clarify something. It occurred to me that the burning bush did not say, "I am Allah," rather, it said, "Moses, I am your Lord..."

A: Yes, in a way the tree spoke to them and said, "O Adam and Eve! You may know everything, but the fulfillment of the duty to *teach* what you know is contingent on making this mistake. So come and steal fruit from me; make a mistake in order to learn what you know." To know is not enough. A person has to become one with knowledge and embody it. This is why God became manifest in the tree, (so as to enable Adam and Eve to learn what they knew). And in doing so, it was as if God secretly told Adam and Eve, "Do not go higher than the station of intellect to the station of love lest your souls be tormented by the immense trial and tribulation you will encounter at that higher station."

Q: Was Adam punished because after being made the site of manifestation for God's essence, he approached the tree of love and became attached to the attributes?

A: Very true. From the essence, he became attached to the attributes. And perhaps it is on account of his going back from the essence to the attributes that Iqbal says, "The pleasure of paradise was inscribed in his heart, when he himself was the essence and paradise. This is why he was cast out." But in my opinion, Adam did not commit a sin. He did what he had to do, and this is how he came to acknowledge his own non-existence and nothingness. To reach the point of realizing our non-existence and say, "We don't exist," we must first commit mistakes and errors. I was recently speaking to a friend who said, "I used to love drinking (alcohol), but I gave it up; was my act of giving up the habit more worthy to God than the restraint of a person who never drank?" Of course not. You will make mistakes – accept that you have made mistakes, and then refrain from them for God. In the eyes of God, restraint and renouncement for His sake is admirable, because it requires struggle and effort. And God loves the struggle and effort of human beings when it is for His sake. Consider two individuals that profess their love for each other, but are unable to make any sacrifices for the other. Can this be called love? No, it cannot. Similarly, simply saying, "O God, I love You!" is not enough. The real question is how much are you able and prepared to sacrifice for your beloved? Do you fear that you might lose your beloved? Our relationship with and love for God should produce these concerns. Going back to Adam and Eve, it is as if God spoke those words to Adam. It is also as if God made human beings capable of and passionately inclined towards love, and pushed them towards it. Let us connect this point with the poem of Kenan Rifa'i. Wasn't a similar thing said to Husayn, the Adam of his time? Most certainly, he was told, "Dear son, don't proceed, else you will suffer immensely!" But just like Adam, Husayn too chose non-existence and nothingness. He chose to die for his beloved, and by doing so he chose to set an example for all believers. We are so fortunate to have such lovers of God, who make it possible for us to reach this understanding.

The divine judgments inscribed in the heavenly spheres and the stars are also inscribed in the Preserved Tablet and in God's Book. All of pre-eternity and eternity can be found in the Preserved Tablet and in God's Book, and the ink of the pen has run dry. Sura *An'am* (Livestock) says, "... nor is there a single grain in the darkness of the earth, or anything, fresh or withered, that is not written in a clear Record."[5] So if everything is in God's book, then the conflicting states of hardship and comfort, happiness and oppression, goodness and evil, are all inevitable. We must experience these through the course of our lives. Why? We cannot say, "Why does evil exist?" It exists so that goodness can manifest. Similarly, for God to manifest Himself, non-existence is necessary. All things are known through their opposite.

Some questions might be raised: "What is the purpose of prophetic teachings?" "What are the benefits of prescriptions by doctors or the wisdom of sages?" "If everything is written in God's book and is inevitable, why do we find the unjust shedding of blood due to ignorance and disorder?" I have tried to answer these questions, but let me elaborate further with the help of some examples. The divine judgments that are inscribed in the heavens and the stars are not particular (cüz'i hükumler). Rather, those laws are universal (külli hükumler). Similarly, in this world, the manifestations of the movements of heavenly spheres and stars are not circumscribed, but universal. Moreover neither are the effects of the events caused by the movements of heavenly spheres and stars localized. To the contrary, again, those effects are universal.

Thus when it comes to specific human actions, humans have the prerogative to choose. We decide what to strive towards and what to refrain from. As we said earlier, if we struggle in the way of God, He is content with us and through this we are able to realize our own meaning. Think of it this way: when the sun comes up, it radiates its light on everything equally. It cannot shine its light on some and not on others. At the same time, though, the sun does enable the maturation and ripening of some things, and the burning of others. Apply this analogy to our discussion: when the sun of God's meaning rises, it can either cause us to mature and ripen, or to burn. The outcome depends on our abilities and inclinations. As Yunus Emre (d. 720/1320)[6] once said, "It is love that makes people crazy; it is love that brings disgrace on people." What was he trying to say? That love is at once love and fire. While it can strike one person and raise their station, on striking another person, it

---

5. Qur'an, al-An'am (Livestock), (6:59). Tr. Haleem, The Qur'an, p. 84.

6. Yunus Emre, popular Anatolian Turkish mystic and poet of the fourteenth century.

can make them lustful and lead to their downfall. So under God's meaning, the orientation of each person corresponds to his or her abilities. People are affected by the same events in different ways, in accordance with their different abilities.

Q: What are the factors that affect a person's "ability"?

A: A good person is good from the time they are in their mother's womb. The same is true for a bad person. The world is made up of these two groups. A good person refers to the lover of God. It refers to the person who struggles to reach God's beauty. God manifests Himself through this type of person. A bad person means "sealed." About this type, God says, "I manifest in these individuals as a drop, not as a whole." Bad people exist in this world so that the good can be distinguished. They (the bad) carry no additional burdens for their sins. They will be given no other punishment. Their punishment is already with them. Consider the following story: when the donkey was taken to paradise, it said, "Hee haw hee haw!" When it was taken to hell it said the same thing. On hearing this the people protested, "This donkey doesn't understand a thing!" God replied, "When the donkey is already carrying its punishment on itself, why are you trying to recompense it further?" The point of the story is this: say a man has a problem with another man and is constantly causing him trouble, to the point where all day he burns in the fire of his own jealousy. He is, at the very least, absolutely miserable. His entire day is spent in pain, as he conspires new ways to cause harm to others. Why would I need to curse such a person when he cannot be any worse off than he already is? He lacks the happiness and peace that I possess; he is in so much pain and discomfort.

The person who submits to God is happy and at peace; he remains unfazed by whatever may happen in this world. In contrast, those who do not submit are constantly burdened by worldly trials and tribulations. They are always in pain, and they themselves become a source of many other problems. I still remember once a woman said to me, "I have a weakness for jewelry; I envy even the tiniest piece of artificial jewelry you wear!" This person carries the weight of her troubles with her, and this constantly eats away at her peace. Perfected Humans show the true path to (less perfect) people like us who vacillate between peace and unrest. They serve as a reminder of the right path for us. Did the blessed

Prophet ever give up on Abu Jahl?[7] Never. Didn't he know that Abu Jahl would never believe? He did. But it was as if he had resolved the following: "It is my responsibility to perform my (prophetic) duty as well as possible. The rest is in the hands of God." So Perfected Humans convey and enjoin the good and what is true, as does the Qur'an. However, each person understands what is taught to him/her according to his/her own disposition.

With some people, the offering of sound advice produces the opposite effect; it increases their disbelief and makes them protest and say things like, "who do you think you are to teach me?" Whereas others would say, "everything I learn is beneficial for me; God has graced me with yet another meaning." The objector, or the one who says, "who do you think you are to teach me" is already in hell, while the one who embraces learning is in heaven. There is a lot of talk about terrorists these days. People endlessly ask and wonder, "Will they go to heaven or hell?" "Are they really killing people in the path of God?" It is so tragic that today, when the word Muslim is mentioned, terrorist is what comes to people's minds. This is so painful. The West supports this, and that is how they want a Muslim to be portrayed. Terrorists are already in hell while they are still in this world. If a terrorist hadn't already created hell for himself in this world, would they ever be able to detonate all those bombs? If a person has entered hell while still in this world, is it possible for them to go to paradise in the next world? If we are in peace, and if we are in the presence of God, it means that we are in paradise. If we are not in the presence of God, and are unhappy, we are in hell. If we are in hell, there is a Qur'anic verse urging us to return to the presence of God. It says: "...give alms..." that is, join spiritual discourses, be a service to humanity again, and save yourself from the hellfire. For us to leave this world is like the setting of the sun in this world, only to rise again in the afterlife. This means that the state in which you leave this world is the same state in which you will be resurrected. Thus it can be said that people have the option of being good or bad. All prophets struggle to remind humanity of the right path and lead them to God's presence. Everything inscribed in the Preserved Tablet will become manifest. In this regard, people do not make choices; they are not free. Whatever is written in the heavenly spheres and stars

---

7. Abu Jahl (d. 13/635) is a reference to one of the fiercest opponents and persecutors of the Prophet Muhammad and the early community of believers.

is God's decree. The effects that are manifested through the heavenly spheres and stars are God's destiny.

If a person wants to construct a mill, they first decide where to put it up and think of the materials needed, like a stone, a wheel, and water. After this they obtain the materials, prepare what is needed for rotation, and then grind the flour. Note that there are three steps. First one must think of what materials to use; this is the decree, after which the person struggles to build. But first, it has to be imagined and planned. This act of imagining or picturing is the decree. Doing what is necessary for the decree to be carried out is destiny. The flour that is obtained at the end is also destiny. In the same way, God's knowledge about the heavenly spheres, stars, elements and nature is His decree. God's creation of these heavenly spheres, elements and nature is His decree. The manifestation of the heavens and stars in this world as they start to turn is God's destiny. Stars have a certain effect on us in this world, both inwardly and outwardly. In reality, all the planets and stars that appear to be outside exist in us. Horoscopes and stars affect us. This should not be interpreted – as is often done today – as the telling of fortunes. A Perfected Human comes, takes you from one sphere to another and directs you to the right path. This means that God has programmed you in a certain way in your creation. If your decree is to become wheat, He causes you to be born in a season that will help you manifest your wheat-ness. That season is your horoscope. The wind and the rain of that season help you acquire the required level of maturity as "wheat."

The spiritual disposition with which you are born will enable you, through your efforts, to attain that maturity. Even before you have a need for water, a spiritual teacher guides you to the water. This is what is most crucial. God grants His creatures what is required and desired by their abilities. He assigns to them the appropriate name as their destiny; human form, spirit, abilities, and attitude are written in the sperm of humans. People are bound to exist in their own form and spirit. They will necessarily have the abilities that they have, but they are free in their actions. So, while decree is predetermined, our destiny is determined by our actions. People say, "Your destiny is in your hands" without reflecting on what this means. Destiny is the fulfillment of decree. And the way our destiny is lived out is in our hands.

Q: Could you please explain this with an example for us to understand it better?

A: Let's say it is in a person's destiny to become a beautiful person. But trial and difficulty is also written for that person for the sake of their perfection. If they endure the trials and show contentment, that destiny will make them beautiful. If on the other hand they get stuck in a state where with each difficulty and affliction they question, "Why has this happened to me?" then trial and difficulty will not work to perfect them. Instead, they will remain "unripe." This is why we must learn to be content with everything that happens to us. The things that happen to us change our inner structure. They transform us into diamonds when we are just carbon and coal. If instead of transforming into diamonds we insist on staying as coal and say, "No, I will not suffer any pain in this world!" then we will remain at the level of coal. But if we are content with suffering, and if we treat pain not as pain but as a sign that the Beloved is with us, and if when difficulties arise we are able to say, "Praise be to God, this is from my beloved; He has considered me worthy of this, and He has loved me," then difficulties will become delights that transform us into diamonds. To be clear, I am not suggesting that we ask for hardship. I am talking about hardship that is already present and destined to occur.

Q: To be content with our destiny is the goal we should strive for, but how do we get to that station? How can an ordinary person get there?

A: Everything comes down to "love." Spiritual discourses (sohbet) held by Sufis are there to increase our love; we need these discourses in order to realize our love. Spiritual discourse is needed to nourish a person's love. What feeds love are the feelings a person has during a spiritual discourse. All our talk and discussion about love thus far has the same objective: to understand the meaning of God, to find that Beloved in ourselves, to unite with that Beloved, to meet with that Beloved, and to take each breath with the Beloved. The highest form of love is needed to achieve this, that is, to be content with everything, and to view every event as beautiful. Even when it is human love directed towards a man or a woman, if the beloved scolds the lover, the lover derives pleasure from this. Why? "Because they have spoken to me!" is the answer. It seems "they were upset by something I did." When someone is reproached by their intimate friend, they experience much pleasure, and think, "if this person hadn't loved me, they would not have reproached me!" Only an immature soul resents being reproached. But can the reproach of a true friend upset us? The reproach of a friend makes us happy. "If they hadn't had love for me, they would not have called me," they think. This is how our relationship with God should be. I, too, reflect on this from time to time. When something really difficult happens to me, I tend to say, "My Beloved must have seen me as distinct from others and so He has granted this difficult situation to me. He must love me so He has given me a more difficult test than He has to others." This is the crux of it: to be able to establish a relationship with the Beloved and to welcome whatever He sends us according to the best of our ability. And we should remember that with contentment there is reciprocity, such that after our contentment is the station where God is content with us.

Q: Is it a universal rule that everyone should be content with his or her destiny? Do people really have to be content with everything that happens?

A: It is not easy for everyone to be content. Of course, being content with our destiny is tied to our abilities. It is related to the pre-eternal decree that is in the self. In fact, the best way for us to establish a relationship with God is to never judge the way others are content with their own destinies. Everybody is pleased to the extent that accords with his or her capacity. It is possible that no one will be content in the way that I am, and I will not be content in the way that others are. I have said this many times already. A very close friend of mine in Konya buried his ten children in a collapsed building last Eid. Can I ask, "Why can't I be like him?" He has met the destiny that was decided for him in pre-eternity by God and God has made it easy on him. We might all see his situation the same way, and after acquiring a lot of information we might learn how to behave in such a situation. But when we actually confront that trial, how do we respond? That's the question. How we respond is related to the favors that God has bestowed on us. So while the extent of our contentment corresponds to our capacity, the ability to respond well and to be content is only possible through God's help and blessing. We respectfully bow before those who have such contentment.

Human beings act on their own spiritual predispositions. Did I say human beings? Sorry, every created being in the world acts on its destiny and fate. Let me illustrate this with a story. A mosquito approached the Prophet Solomon to register a complaint. "I'm so upset by this wind! Its continuous blowing is nearly killing me as it forces me along! Could you have a word with it so that it starts to show me some respect?" Solomon speaks to the wind, warning it that it might kill the mosquito, and suggests that it be calmer. The wind replies, "O master! Movement is part of my constitution; it is how I was created. The same God that created me also commanded me to move. I simply obey the command; I don't know what is or is not driven along by my movement. And there is nothing wrong in this because it is ultimately God that has mandated that I, the wind, be blowing." From this story we see that everything has a duty in this world. For some, this duty entails movement, which can be destructive, but it is their duty.

Such people destroy everything in their path without pausing to think about the consequences. Others courteously welcome all things and treat them with love. In sum, every created being will carry out its duty. It is not our place to ask, "Why is such and such person doing this or that?" Our ability to be content with the destiny that God has written for this world rests on our ability to be content with how others will behave according to their own disposition. People are predestined to do what they do; it is their duty. You might do something good for someone, and they might be hostile in response. It is not my place to question this. The goal is to respect what others do. Now, you might ask, "Why do evil-doers get punished if everyone is responsible for doing their duty?" My teacher says, "This brings up a very subtle point." God has opposite names: names that involve the granting of greatness and dignity, and names that cause abasement and despicability. With some of His names He guides and with other of His names He leads astray. He forgives, but He also takes revenge and punishes. All His names came into this world after their pleading with Him, saying, "O God, please grant us a body." When there is suffering and oppression, God sends a person who will carry the name of vengeance. To eliminate the qualities that lead one to oppress others, it is necessary for the person with those qualities to encounter vengeance. When they meet, the two names will control and discipline each other. That's it.

Q: Thank you so much.

Chapter Four:
Divine Unity (*Tevhid*)

Q: What is divine unicity (*tevhid*)?

A: *Tevhid* is a difficult concept to grasp. To reach an adequate understanding of *tevhid*, tremendous striving is needed from the individual. *Tevhid* means to reach the station of seeing God's Names and Attributes everywhere and in everything. Whoever attains this knowledge like 'Ali did, sees God in created things. When 'Ali would hear the sound of a bell he would stop to listen. People asked, "What are you doing, O Imam? It's just the sound of a bell!" He replied, "Look how beautifully the bell chants 'Allah, Allah.'"

 Tevhid is to be able to see God's self-disclosure (*tecelli*) in everything – note that I did not say "Allah" but His "self-disclosure" – in beauty and blessings, pain and severity, plants and animals. *Tevhid* is to feel that the work of the Divine is in all things, so *tevhid* is the ability to love all things. As Yunus Emre said, "I love the created for the sake of the Creator." By this he meant that he saw Him in everything, and loved Him in everything. *Tevhid* is the beginning and the end of everything. Pre-eternity and eternity begin with *tevhid*. We manifest from the One, as per the scientific principle established by Lavoisier:[1] "Nothing comes into existence from absolute non-existence, and nothing falls into absolute non-existence once it exists." Everything comes from the One and returns to the One.

---

1. Antoine-Laurent de Lavoisier (d. 1794), French nobleman and chemist, widely known as the "father of chemistry."

Q: Does *tevhid* mean to come from the Everliving (*Hayy*) and to return to "He" (*Hu*)?[2]

A: Yes; *tevhid* begins with the journey of coming from the Everliving (*Hayy*) and choosing to go back to He (*Hu*). At each moment, with each breath that we take, God says to us "I exist." God says "*Hayy*," and revives us. If we use our breath in the right way and send it back to Beauty, to *Hu*, then in one moment our breath comes from *Hayy* and goes to *Hu*. It comes from and returns to *tevhid*.

How should we understand and reach *tevhid*? Let me try to explain through a simple story from Paul Coelho's novel, *The Devil and Miss Prym*, in which he recounts a tale about Leonardo da Vinci. The cardinals of the time ask Leonardo to paint "The Last Supper" of Jesus. He gladly accepts and starts to search for men who might resemble the image of Judas and Jesus that he had in mind for his painting. To match his image of Jesus, he searches for a young, radiant fellow. He quickly spots someone who matches this description in a church choir. The young gentleman whom he selects has a truly angelic and luminous face. As for Judas' character, he is on the lookout for an unsightly face. After continuing to search for five long years, he is left disappointed and unsuccessful. Of course the cardinals, who had anxiously been waiting for the painting to receive its final touches, are livid. Having reached their wits end, they shout at him for his inability to complete the painting. But just the previous day, Leonardo had come across a drunkard whose face was very ugly. He'd thought to himself, "Finally, I found him! His is truly an ugly face, fitting with Satan's!" He moved quickly and started to paint Judas before the man could wake up from his deep sleep. But just as he was completing his painting, the drugged-looking man woke up. And to Leonardo's surprise, he claimed to recognize Leonardo's painting. Of course Leonardo was shocked, but also excited: "How can you say you recognize what no one has ever seen? You must have just heard about this project, and now you think you recognize it." But the man was adamant: "Absolutely not. I am certain that I know this painting. Don't you remember, five years ago, you used a young radiant model from

---

2. "The Everliving" (*Hayy*) is one of the ninety-nine names of God. The pronoun "He" (*Hu*) in Sufi literature signifies the essence of God and succinctly captures the idea of God as the singular source of all existence. It is used similarly in the Qur'an, as in the formula: "There is no god but He (*la ilaha illa hu*)" Qur'an 2:163.

the church choir to paint Jesus? That was me."

This story teaches us that beauty and ugliness are one and the same. And, similarly, Majesty and Beauty are the manifestations of God seen through different mirrors. Maybe there is no good or evil, no beauty or ugliness; rather, these are just projections that appear in varying degrees and amounts. At an amusement park we find those distorted mirrors that reflect us as taller, shorter, fatter, and thinner than we actually are. The person being reflected doesn't change even as the reflections change according to the mirror. Similarly, this world is a series of God's appearances in different mirrors. And the very purpose of our creation is to see the reflection of God's Beauty in those mirrors.

Perhaps the best parable for this is in the *Mathnawi*, as I mentioned earlier. Once, the ruling king set up two teams from among the Mongols and the Turks and organized a painting competition. Each team was directed to a massive wall, which they were instructed to paint. A curtain was drawn in between to prevent either team from seeing the other's work. The Mongols did a tremendous job using all kinds of vivid colors that blended into one another. The Turks however, kept on carving and polishing. Finally, the curtain was removed. What did they see? The brilliant Mongol painting was reflected on the Turks' wall, and appeared even more stunning than it actually was! Similarly, this world was created due to God's desire to see His Eternally Beautiful appearance on the carved and polished walls of our souls. The people of unicity (*ahl-e-tevhid*) have the capacity to see and understand this; they see His reflection in many places.

> Q: So in order to witness and testify, we have to be from among the people of *tevhid*. In order to become Muslim and submit, we say, "I bear witness that there is no god but God" (*ashhadu anna la ilaha illa'Llah*) (which is the proclamation of *tevhid*). What is the meaning of this proclamation?

A: All of creation has come to this world only to understand the secret of this sentence. Why? Because the world is composed of two categories: "Creation" (*halk*; Ar. *khalq*) and "Truth" (*Hakk*; Ar. *Haqq*). Creation struggles in this world to find the secret. That is, in order to reach the Preserved Tablet assigned to them as their lot in pre-eternity, people are perpetually in a state of struggle, knowingly or unknowingly. Through their struggle, they constantly negate the "L," or *"la,"* which is non-existence. In other words, they discipline their *nefis*, which is at the station of the letter L. With the disciplining of this L, extreme desire and lust are pacified. The *nefis* becomes *Hakk*, which is to say that it reaches its essence; rightness manifests and transforms into *Hakk*. So in the phrase, *"La ilaha illa'Llah"* (there is no god but God), *La* means to destroy! Destroy what? The self-worshipping part of *nefis*. If you do so, the Truth will begin to manifest in you. If you pronounce, *"La ilaha"* (there is no god), and understand that you are not a deity, you become *"illa'Llah"* (except God). God alone will manifest in you. If you saw this in everything, you would testify that God manifests Himself in those who destroy their *nefis*. You would say, "I know and see that God manifests in those who purified their existence from their *nefis*." This is the foundation of witnessing. Witnessing is the only path to *tevhid*. Whatever else we worship is false and an idol. Toppling such idols is what is most crucial.

The meaning of this proclamation of *tevhid* is to destroy our egotistical selves, our *nefis*, our extreme desires, and our self-worshipping. Why must we do this? Ibn 'Arabi says, "In their personality, humans carry both lordship and servitude." What does this mean? Let's look at humans. What makes up a human being? The ego-self or soul (*nefis*), the spirit (*ruh*), the intellect, and the heart. Humans are made up of these four parts. The *ruh* is the secret of God. It is not created. It is a manifestation of the Creator. The *nefis* is a creation and is therefore a servant. It is the part which says "I." It represents a manifestation of the earth. It also comes from God, it comes from the Universal Soul, but it is separated, and subordinate to earth. All kinds of lust, hatred, vengeance, and desire have accumulated in the *nefis*. When the *nefis* is active in the body, when it is managing the intellect with all its hatred and vengeance, we might say that the animal spirit dominates the body. Now, when the divine light of God reflects on the piece of flesh that is called "the heart," it transforms into the enlightened or knowing heart. This divine light also falls on the intellect. When this happens, the intellect calls out to the *nefis*, saying, "You have ruled me all this time, but you are bound for non-existence. You are mortal. There is the *ruh*, which is eternal in the body. It has more rights over you. Therefore, from now on, struggle with your own self!" With the assistance and guidance of the intellect, the *nefis* starts to destroy the head of excessive desires. In this [struggle], its greatest supporter is love (*aşk*). When the *nefis* comes to realize its inherent non-existence and nothingness, and when it realizes that it was created for servitude, the *ruh* establishes its dominance in the body. Therefore, Yunus Emre's saying, "There is inside me an 'I' within my 'I'," means there is a spiritual "I" in the animal "I." Make the spiritual "I" rule, make it dominant!

Q: What does "He who knows himself, knows his Lord" mean?[3]

A: For the one who knows his *nefis* or his nothingness, his *ruh* enters the station of *Rabb* (lordship), which is the station of the Teacher. All of this takes place in the human being. The person who attains servitude is able to say, "I am incapable and powerless, I know nothing; everyone has higher qualities than me." This person becomes subservient to his spirit and its teaching, and begins to be trained by it.

Q: Both Pharaoh and Nimrod asserted, "Indeed, I am the mightiest lord!" And for this they received God's curse. Meanwhile, friends of God like Mansur Hallaj and Bayezid Bistami said, "I am the Truth." Can you explain the difference between these two statements?

A: No created being in the entire cosmos has ever tried to claim lord-like authority for itself except the human being. Because of the inclination for sovereignty in him, the human being made the claim to lord-like authority. If this claim is made before the eye of the heart has fully opened to the divine, then the body comes under the control of the *nefis* and the person will be afflicted with misfortune. They will become arrogant, self-righteous, selfish, and outwardly powerful, but remain weak and fragile on the inside. Such people appear to be strong and dominant, but they are vulnerable and susceptible to being destroyed by the smallest of things. Let alone a major upheaval, they are unable to withstand the slightest shock. They begin to struggle with their *nefis*. When they feel that the absolute Truth inheres in and reflects from them, and that lordship has entered their spirits, they begin to struggle with their *nefis*. They say, I reached the Truth; that is what was required of me. I realized it, that is, I became "*Ene'l Hak* (I am the Truth)."

---

3. The quotation refers to a *Hadith Qudsi*, a narration or report that relates the words of God in the first person.

Q: They don't say, "I am God," instead they say, "I am the Truth."

A: They don't say, "I am God." Rather, their statement implies the following: "I reached my own truth, I have become the Truth; my truth has become manifest, because this is what God asked of me; I battled with my *nefis*, and shouted out my servitude." In other words, while saying that they are the Truth, they are saying that they are perfect servants.

Q: In *Fihi Ma Fihi*, Mevlana Rumi says, "When Mansur uttered the words, 'I am the Truth,' he was actually saying, 'I have annihilated myself, and what is left of me is only the Truth.'" Is Mevlana Rumi suggesting that Mansur's state is that of humility?

A: Very much so. It is a form of humility, and is certainly not arrogance. He didn't claim to be God. People who were unable to comprehend Mansur's words later said to him, "Set aside this pretense of claiming to be God and avoid punishment!" He replied, "Whoever said that should take it back because I never said such a thing." To be the truth is to say, "I was the truth in the sense that I struggled with my *nefis*, and I wish everyone was able to do what I did." Do you know what Mansur's mistake was? He hastened to proclaim that he was the truth in front of those who were not. Had he not, they might not have reacted in the way they did. This is why Mevlana Rumi says in the *Mathnawi*, "The world is composed of different groups: the first group hears about the sea's existence. They hear of it, but never see it. They only know of it through knowledge. A second group of people see the sea, become the eye of certainty, love it, enjoy it, they even touch it with their hands and shout 'I am united with the sea, I know the sea.' They shout like Mansur Hallaj. Then there is a third group of people, like myself, lost at sea, annihilated in it, consumed in it, they don't even open their mouths, they have no power to speak or to make any claims." These are the different stations between the friends of God. Those who know *tevhid* only through knowledge lament, "I long to see God in everything, but I continue to get upset and break down." Those who see *tevhid* shout, "I see God in everything!" And those who are annihilated in *tevhid* cannot find the words to speak. What claims can they make and what can they pursue, given that everything is Him? Therefore, theirs is a truly sublime station.

Q: In that case, can it also be said that the "people of *tevhid*" are the "people of silence?"

A: People of *tevhid* are people of silence in two ways: inwardly and outwardly. They keep silent, no one can make them gossip or speak ill of anyone. They have no airs about them; if they did, before whom would they make their claims? God? Who would they gossip about or speak ill of? God? 'Abd al-Karim al-Jili, who was from among the people of *tevhid* said, "In the *hadith* of the Prophet it is said, 'The alms that you give fall into the hand of God before they touch the palm of the person to whom they are given.' Everything is a manifestation from God." He stresses this further by asking, "When you shout at someone, don't your bitter words reach God first before smacking your opponent in the face? Does this not cause you to feel shame?"

Q: A human being is the only created being who makes claims to lordship while at the same time also claiming to be a servant. What is the difference between these?

A: God says that only the human being was created with His Beauty and Majesty. In some people. only majesty manifests, such as in Pharaoh who claimed, "I am god." In others, God's beauty manifests, such as in the Prophet who said, "O God, I haven't come to know You the way You should be known." From among all of God's creation, the human being is very important because both divine majesty and divine beauty manifest in him. God wants His servants to be similar to Him, for them to unite majesty and beauty, and for them to cover the majesty with their beauty; God desires such servants and calls them the people of completion (*sahib-e-kemal*). He desires servants with beautiful traits, who cover their anger with mercy. He doesn't want any "gods" or "goddesses" together with Himself. Let us remember what God said to Moses, "Tell My servant that we both say I; for his sake I would not exist, but I can't not exist as I am the Everliving, the source of all life. So he must come to Me with My opposite, or non-existence; he should come to Me with self-negation and annihilation."

Q: Completion occurs when majesty and beauty come together in human beings. You explained this concept earlier while discussing the divine name "Beauty." After going through these various stages, a person's identity, or *"hu"* (he), comes through.

God brings a person to life with the name "Everliving;" does this mean that after going through these stages, that person comes to possess his own identity and character?

A: Yes; in order for a person to have character, his spirit must become the lord and his *nefis* the servant. After training and disciplining the *nefis,* it is possible to see that God manifests through the self. But what does this "seeing" entail? People should not get angry, resentful, upset, irritated, or offended; instead, they must remember that all things are God, and when inclined to anger they must ask, "How can I possibly get angry with my God, my Beloved?" They must learn to see Him just like Majnun (Qays) saw Leyla. How did Majnun see Leyla? The story begins with Leyla, the daughter of a king, who was serving food to some workers – Majnun was from among them. She served the food to all the workers except Majnun. When his turn came and he held out his plate, instead of serving him, Leyla hit his plate with the spoon. Majnun was bowled over by this gesture. But his friends were skeptical. They said, "Hey, she didn't give you any food. If she were actually in love with you, she would have given you plenty!" Majnun replied, "Why should she treat me the same way as you? To treat me differently was her way of displaying her love for me." We must bring ourselves to say, "How beautiful that God trusts that I will show patience and survive this. That is why He treats me differently." And it is the same logic that we should apply when people get angry with us. We should treat such moments as opportunities for feeling the presence of God and seeing His manifestation as a way of overcoming a difficult test.

Q: There is another saying of Mevlana Rumi, where he says "*La ilaha illa'Llah* (there is no god but God)" is *tevhid* for lay believers, whereas *tevhid* for the spiritual elite is "*La ilaha illa Hu* (there is no god but He)."

A: "*Hu* (He)" means that there is only He, nothing else. He is distant from us, but at the same time He manifests in us and in every place. Now there are two critical concepts: incomparability (*tenzih*) and similarity (*teshbih*). Understanding these is important. *Tenzih* means to know God's oneness, His indivisibility, the indescribability of His divine nature, the fact that "He does not beget nor was He begotten," and the knowledge that He is greater and loftier than all things. *Teshbih* means to know that He manifests in all things and to respect all things due to His manifestation (in them). When the knowledge of a person occupies a place between *tenzih and teshbih*, he becomes a Perfected Human.

Q: If God manifests in all things, then why is it that people's love for their children, money, or for themselves is seen as a claim to Lordship and not as servitude to God?

A: Money and other similar things are nothing more than a means. To be able to see God's manifestations is one thing, but to be in awe of His grandeur and absolute Supremacy is quite another. Adam's example is relevant here. How can we bring ourselves to see God in the parts, that is, through His attributes, in the same way that Adam did? While the individual parts do not represent God in totality, they can still serve as a means to access that totality. God is the (indivisible) whole. Let me explain this through an example. Consider a rose. The petals and colors of the rose are its attributes. It might be red or yellow, or even black or blue (that is how they make them these days). If our eyes are closed, in order for us to gauge whether a rose is there, we have to use our sense of smell. God's meaning is this fragrance. His manifestations in us are the petals, colors and names. If we get stuck with one name though, we will be like a hunter who wastes his bullets on the shadow of a bird rather than the bird itself. Let me explain this in another way. Imagine a shadow play (*Karagöz*).[4] The same person behind the curtain performs every character in a *Karagöz* play. The *Karagöz* master plays the villain, the beautiful girl, the neighborhood's busybody, the gypsy... and so on. If we treat the different characters as separate individuals, and forget the sole source of the power behind the curtain, then we get angry with the witch who separates the beautiful girl from her lover. Whereas the one who understands the reality laughs at us and says, "These fools are stuck outside the curtain; don't they recognize the real power behind all these characters?" This is what it's all about. Our puppet strings are in the hands of that Majestic Director. He has assigned different roles to each of us on this world's stage, but it is He who plays and speaks through all the characters. If we were to take a gun and shoot the witch because she was causing pain to the girl and the boy, peo-

---

4. The principal character in the Turkish shadow play, and also the shadow play theatre itself.

ple would laugh! Yet we make this mistake so often. We shout and swear at people when they overtake us in traffic. We get upset at people with different viewpoints. Instead of resolving such challenges with love, and instead of seeing His manifestation in all things, we make a mockery of ourselves by mistreating others.

Q: There is another very good example of this in Rumi's *Fihi Ma Fihi*. He says, "If wind blows in the palace, the corner of the rug flutters, leaves and dust fly around, ripples form in the pool, and tree branches sway back and forth. These are all different states but they all result from the wind."

A: Also the story in the *Mathnawi* which I previously mentioned: a mosquito complains about the wind to Solomon, saying, "It blows so powerfully that each time I am shaken to the core of my being. Soon it will destroy me! Please instruct it to slow down." On hearing the mosquito's plea, Solomon summons the wind and says, "Why do you scare the mosquito?" The wind replies, "Of that I am not aware. God tells me to move, so I do. I don't notice what things I carry with me when I obey His command. My duty is to move, and I fulfill it without any questioning."

We must not be like that mosquito when confronted with a person whose duty is to move. We should be strong. And to be strong we need to work on our character. Whoever is subdued by his *nefis* is doomed to fail. One of the best models of strong character is Diogenes. I have already mentioned this story, but let me tell it again. Diogenes said to Alexander, "You think you have a strong character? You are the slave of my slave." When asked what he meant by that, he replied, "I have subdued my ego-self and made it a perfect slave. But you are a slave of that slave; you always say 'I.'" My teacher said that Diogenes was a man of character and Alexander was the one who lacked it. This is why to be strong means to overcome our *nefis*. This is the only way to understand *"La ilaha illa'Llah."*

Q: I just remembered a *hadith qudsi* in which God says, "My servant draws near to Me through supererogatory works until I love him. Then, when I love him, I am his hearing through which he hears, his sight through which he sees, and his tongue with which he speaks." I wonder if the people of *tevhid* see the Truth only once they reach God?

A: Very true. First, keep in mind that the people of *tevhid* are those for whom the attainment of this station was preordained in pre-eternity. In other words, a person needs a pre-eternal guarantee that declares that he is not foolish. We should talk about foolishness, since it is not what we associate it with these days. Second, some effort has to be demonstrated. The entire world is based on these two things: the allocation of one's lot in pre-eternity, and a person's exertion of his own effort. God does not like those who say things like, "A lover of God prayed for me, so I am exalted!" God loves effort. Let me explain this with an example from the *Mathnawi*: "Moses and Pharaoh placed a bet, where Moses said to Pharaoh, "Let's see which one of us can make the Nile flow upstream tomorrow." Moses assumed that God would support him, since he was, after all, a prophet. He slept comfortably that night, having adopted an attitude similar to people who would say, "(the protection of) such and such saint surrounds me." Meanwhile, Pharaoh pleaded with God during the night, saying, "O Lord! I ask you by Your grace to help me; I know that You are God, but people insist on pronouncing me as God and I can't undo my claim to Lordship! This is the reason for my not having become a servant! Please help me!" The following morning, it was Pharaoh who made the Nile flow upstream. Moses was totally bewildered, and on asking God about the meaning behind this, he received the following reply: "O Moses, yes, you are indeed My messenger, but that should not have prevented you from struggling and supplicating Me. You did not exert yourself at all, while that poor Pharaoh pleaded with Me and took refuge from his misery and helplessness; he struggled and toiled, so I helped him."" As this story makes clear, we must constantly strive to make an effort.

Q: We were discussing "foolishness," and you said for a person to progress they have to get past their foolishness. How is this done?

A: It is impossible to escape foolishness for those whose fates have been consigned to that condition. No matter what they do, they are unable to rid themselves of their foolishness. What's more, they end up striving in ways that exacerbate the foolishness that afflicts them. But what is this foolishness? It is the condition of remaining unaware of why one was created. It is to be oblivious of God's all-encompassing existence, despite all the signs of His presence before one's eyes. Such awareness lends a person a completely new lens with which to view the world; in the absence of this lens, the heart remains constricted, ignorant of God's existence. This is what generates foolishness. An excellent example that illustrates this point is in Mevlana's *Fihi Ma Fihi*. He says, "A group of teachers taught a child different subjects and skills, including fortune telling. The child advanced so far in his learning that eventually, he knew everything. The teachers then decided to test him. One of them took a ring, covered it with his hand, and asked the child to guess its contents. The child who knew everything said you have something circular, hollow and yellow in your hand. The teachers were extremely proud of this mature and clever student. When they asked him to specify what this circular, hollow and yellow thing was, the child took some time to think it over before replying, "It is a sieve, master!" Did you follow the moral of the story? An extremely knowledgeable child – one who is even able to predict what a thing is without seeing it – failed when he relied on reason to determine the answer. He was unable to figure out that a sieve does not fit in the palm of one's hand. This is what I mean by foolishness. People might study and master a thousand subjects, but because of their foolishness they don't recognize that the purpose of knowledge is to bring them closer to God. Now if the veil of this foolishness were to be lifted, what would they be able to see? They would see the completeness of God; His presence. They would see that it is God Who manifests in people and creation. They would see that what comes to be known through scientific knowledge, and everything that is manifest in matter, is God.

When we consider different kinds of bodily diseases, we find that there is no power in our hands and it is God who manifests in this. We see and understand that even an intellectually gifted individual is nothing but a relative projection in an illusory realm. And we see that in addition to this dream-like realm, there exists another world that is invisible to the eye. If knowledge does not bring a person closer to God, then that person is a fool. Meanwhile, if the acquisition of knowledge leads a person to God, then that person is a possessor of wisdom.

Q: Can you say something about the qualities of being miserly and arrogant?

A: The three main obstacles on our path to attaining the state of *tevhid* are: being foolish, miserly, and arrogant. As we said earlier,

106

to be arrogant means to see ourselves as idols. Let me read a passage from the work, *Gulshan-i Raz* (*The Rose Garden of the Secret*):[5]

> Since all things are projections of the One Single Being, they are all ultimately idols. Think straight, intelligent one! In the presence of the One Being, idols are not false. If a disbeliever comes to know the true essence of his idol, he is dumbfounded! The reason for his disbelief is that his vision is limited to the idol's apparent form. If, on the other hand, you are incapable of seeing the truth behind an idol, then as per Islam, you are not a Muslim.

To see only the apparent form of things is to disbelieve and practice dualism. We usually differentiate and say there is God and then there are other things; there is Ahmed, and there is God. But if you see things as manifestations of God and are able to say, "God's majesty has manifested in this poor being, let me not get upset," or "God's beauty has manifested in this poor being, let me be happy!" – that is, if you focus on the painter instead of the painting – then you understand *tevhid*. And what is left for us to then be arrogant about? Once you see that God is manifest in you too, about what will you boast? If He is in everyone and everything, then how can we claim any form of supremacy? My late teacher said, "When I step outside, I see that all things are superior to me." Confused, his companions asked him how this was possible. He replied, "The donkey that passes me in the street can carry a heavier load than me. The cook can prepare better food than me. The housekeeper can clean a house better than me. So how can I be arrogant towards any of them?" He also said, "One day the end of this world will be announced with the sound of the trumpet. At that moment, all worldly hierarchies will be overturned. So what is there that is left to boast about? Indeed, it is from the earth that you were created and to the earth that you will return. Your origin was a drop of dirty water, and your future is a rotting corpse. What is there for you to be haughty about?"

Q: Is it true that the faults we see in others are actually reflections of our own shortcomings?

A: This is very true! The faults we see in others are not unfamiliar to us. It is our own shortcomings that we recognize in other peo-

---

5. Authored by Mahmud Shabistari (d. 720/1320), Persian mystic and poet.

ple, but then we direct our anger towards them. The faults we see are our own. People would be much better off if, during a negative encounter, they were critical of themselves and asked where they themselves went wrong. Let me share a simple story narrated to me by a teacher-friend. During her first year of teaching, the principal of her school asked her to come see him in order to modify her schedule and syllabus. She was very young and arrogant at the time, so she protested, "Why should I go to him? He should come to me; I'm taking a break here!" As it turns out, the principal went to her and apologized, "The reason I sent for you is because I was trying to correct your schedule in order to help you; please forgive me!" The same friend said that she paid the price for her arrogant ways in the last days before her retirement. She said, "I was in my final days before retiring from a small village school when one day the building's janitor approached me and began insulting me in a loud voice. I couldn't understand why. I had always been good to this janitor, yet here he was yelling, 'Get lost! We'll be getting rid of you tomorrow!' That night, I kept replaying this strange encounter in my mind, until it clicked: this was my payback for being arrogant with my principal in my first year of teaching! I was extremely grateful to God for allowing me to settle my accounts before retiring; I prostrated before him in gratitude. Even though at first I didn't understand it, when I realized that God was making me pay for my arrogance, I was grateful." If we all view the world with such a lens, then we will be able to cleanse ourselves of arrogance and self-righteousness. May God grant us such purity.

As for miserliness, it is really one of the worst qualities to have. The entire Qur'an forbids people from it. Miserliness, or the condition of being unable to give, does not just refer to the giving of one's property; to give of our property is our duty and we have to do it. In fact, if someone coerces us to give from our wealth, forget kissing their hands, we should kiss their feet! This is because any and all help that we offer to people is a message from God telling us that He loves us. This kind of giving is obligatory. What I mean by miserliness is the inability to "give away" our bad manners, to hold onto and let our bad manners pile up for ourselves. According to this meaning, to not be miserly means to be like the earth in its humility and like the sun in its generosity. What do we mean by emulating the earth's humility? Let me explain. We discard all kinds of impurities in the earth, we bury our dead in it, and we step on it whenever we please. Yet, its only response is to consistently offer us lush, green vegetation. All our nourishment comes from the earth, and when we die, the earth receives us with an embrace. So to be like the earth in its humility means to give unconditionally, like the sun, which lights up each place in equal amounts, regardless of whether that place is a grand palace or barren ruins. What is more, because the ruins are decrepit, they derive greater benefit from the sun's light. Meanwhile the palace benefits less, as it is much stronger and more arrogant.

Q: Is "a ruined person" someone who has gotten rid of his selfish ambitions and desires?

A: Yes, there are times when we are heartbroken and feel belittled or despised. Such times fill us with sorrow and our hearts become like ruins. An intelligent person, on the other hand, rejoices at such occasions and thinks, "God is with me; praise be to Him that I have been belittled by people; I have been granted my God's love and beauty; how fortunate, what a great blessing!" I also feel immense joy when misfortune hits from time to time and say, "God knows that I have the strength to endure this pain, and He endures this pain with me by manifesting through me. I am a lucky servant!" May God always grant us this understanding so we never perceive pain as pain or trouble as trouble.

Let me return to our earlier discussion on *tevhid*. According to the Şeriat, the human being is created after the eternal being. It is for this reason that the Şeriat states, "Allah is one thing and creation is something else." But if you ask the people of *tevhid*, they say, "The being is One, not two." This singular being has an inner and outer aspect. The light of this universe is like a single ray of light in relation to the sun, or like a single drop of water in relation to the ocean. The point I am trying to make is this: all created things receive divine light. Therefore what radiates from all of existence is the manifestation of this divine light. In this way, the most exalted divine light manifests in this outer structure that is called "being." Yet, it is important to note that if you collect all the light, it doesn't add up to God because God did not apportion His light between us. Rather, the same divine light manifests in each one of us. He reflects the light upon us and makes it manifest. He is the Indivisible Whole. "He begets not, nor is He begotten." All human faculties, including hearing, sight, physical power, and free will are possible through this light, as per the saying of Ibn 'Arabi, "It is I speaking and I listening." There is nothing else in this world other than the Absolute Truth.

Q: Do we need a "friend of God" to establish this oneness in our being?

A: Absolutely. Trying to attain *tevhid* on one's own is like trying to carve a mountain with a needle. How is it that God's friends can help us? They teach us who we really are. They teach us about love, and about how to love. God's friends are not unlike catalysts in a chemical reaction. They play a facilitating role in our journey towards God; they make everything easier, and then leave as if nothing happened. But they keep watching us to make sure that we are on the right track. They never fall into despair or turn away from us because of our mistakes or bad behavior. As the Prophet said to God during his farewell sermon: "I have conveyed all Your words to the people; You know the rest."

Q: Let's continue with *tevhid* in these beautiful days of spring. Earlier, you said, "*Tevhid* is silence." Can you explain this, please?

A: The spring festival, or *Hıdrellez* (Ar. *Khidr-Ilyas*),[6] marks the beginning of spring as the season for renewal. Let me share some thoughts on the inner meaning of *Hıdrellez*. Our topic has been on *tevhid*, and during the *Hıdrellez* another type of *tevhid* or unity takes place. This is the day when the prophets Khidr and Elijah met. Ibn 'Arabi has said that after the Prophet Muhammad, there are always three prophetic stations present in the world: the stations of Enoch (Idris), Elijah (Ilyas), and Jesus.[7] One of these prophets maintains world order; one maintains the meaning

---

6. *Hıdrellez*, in the Turkish tradition, is the name for a popular festival in the spring. Khidr (Tr. *Hızır*) is a figure in the Qur'an who represents a quintessential spiritual guide and possessor of inner knowledge. In the Turkish tradition he also symbolizes the renewal of vegetation in the spring. It is believed that, when this personage shows himself upon the face of the earth, he leaves a green impression on the hands of people, and brings abundance, fertility and happiness. Another feature of his legendary personality is that he comes to the aid of beings in distress. In regard to Ilyas (Elijah), beliefs and traditions surrounding this figure are somewhat rare. In literary texts and in oral tradition there are allusions to his supernatural aid to beings in distress on land or sea. See P.N. Boratav, *Encyclopedia of Islam*, 2nd Edition, s.v. "Hidrelliz," Brill Online, 2012.
7. See Glossary for Elijah and Enoch.

of prophethood in the world, and one maintains the station of sainthood in the world (which is the station of 'Ali). Ibn 'Arabi says that the pole of the time, or the Prophet's successor of the time, holds the station of Khidr, (that is, of sainthood).[8] So the holder of the station of prophethood in the human heart is Elijah, and the one holding the station of sainthood is Khidr.[9] And what is the inner meaning of this? It is that prophethood and sainthood manifest in the human heart. Ibn 'Arabi says that when the spirit becomes the sovereign master and teacher, then in the heart of such a person, spring flowers blossom, and *Hıdrellez* takes place. So, the inner meaning of *Hidrellez* is the arrival of spring in the human heart. For the arrival of spring, the spirit must understand both prophethood and sainthood, and that spirit must train the body through these stations. When the disciplining process culminates in the heart, spring flowers blossom, and beautiful fragrances spread from that person and disperse throughout the world. The person may not be very beautiful in their outer appearance, but their fragrance suffuses the entire world. This is a heavenly fragrance. They asked Majnun one day, "How is it that you are so in love with Leyla when she is a dark, skinny, and ugly girl?" He said, "You only see the goblet, whereas I am still intoxicated by the wine inside."

> Q: Is what you're saying here related to the eye of the heart described by 'Ali when he broke the idols at the Ka'ba and said, "Every place has become the Beauty of the Messenger of God!"?

A: Yes. This is the level of understanding at the station of 'Ali, who taught us to see God's meaning everywhere; he taught us *tevhid*. In order for *tevhid* to settle in a person's heart, they have to purge themselves of all excessive desires and idolatry. But this is only possible with the help of a Perfected Human. A Per-

---

8. In Cemalnur's formulation here, sainthood is equivalent to the figure of Khidr. Hence, Jesus' manifestation in each age is represented by the name Khidr.

9. Here it is important to note that this mention of the human heart should not be taken to mean that these mystical stations solely represent interiorized states detached from the temporal realm. Rather, it is precisely through the material body and actions of the perfect spiritual guide (*al-murshid al-kamil*) who is inspired by the charisma of prophets that the efficacy of these stations is realized. Thus, the coalescence of sainthood and prophethood disrupts the separation between the inner and the outer. *Hidrellez* in this sense is the celebration of the realization of this coalescence.

fected Human projects God's light, or God's meaning, onto our hearts; this light transforms the piece of flesh we call "heart" into a site of divine manifestation, or an illuminated heart. The illuminated heart activates the intellect. The *nefis* begins to understand its own nothingness, and the intellect no longer ascribes any power to the *nefis*. Instead, the intellect attaches itself to the spirit, or to that part of us that is directly from God. Once the spirit takes control, it starts to discipline the body. This process is like the onset of spring in the human heart, and at that time the "people of presence" (the spiritually attuned, or people in the presence of God) become abundantly visible. You will note that *tevhid* and disciplining (*terbiye*) refer to a person's spiritual growth, where the *nefis* is disciplined under the guidance of the spirit. In order for this growth to take place, light is essential. But what is light (*nur*) here? Let me explain the term "*nur*" letter by letter: the letter "n" (*nun*) signifies the first intellect (*akl-ı evvel*; Ar. *al-aql al-awwal*), which is the Muhammadan Truth (*Hakikat-i Muhammadi*). God's words, "I wanted to be known," reflect from Him in all that is beautiful; this is "the Muhammadan Truth." Within this truth is the Preserved Tablet of all that has been created and all that is yet to be created. (The Preserved Tablet consists of the essence of God's Names and Attributes, present in all of creation as God's truth, or the reason for existence). The first intellect is like the sun. The letter "V" (*vav*) (represented by its sound "u" in the word "*nur*"), or "*vilayet*," means the manifestation of God's essence in this universe. It refers to the Perfected Human. The light of God first illuminates Perfected Human beings, and then their light illuminates us. When a person's intellect reaches this level, it is the Universal Intellect (*akl-ı kul*; Ar. *al-aql al-kulli*), which functions as a bridge by which we learn the meaning of the Muhammadan Truth. We only possess worldly intellect (*akl-ı maaş*; Ar. *al-aql al-ma'ashi*). But when a person attaches his intellect – which is but a drop – to the Universal Intellect, or when he considers the intellect of a Perfected Human superior to his own and comes under the command of the Perfected Human's intellect, then the letter "R" (*akl-i maad*; Ar. *al-aql al-ma'adi*) or the intellect of return emerges and reaches maturity. From then on everyone welcomes everything that person does.

Q: For the intellect to be attached to the Universal Intellect, it has to be illuminated by the heart and made aware of the spirit?

A: Yes. An intellect illuminated through the heart and attached to the Universal Intellect is like the letter "V" (*vav*). As the hadith states, the eye with which he sees becomes the Truth; Truth speaks through him. Only beautiful things manifest from such an intellect. And the station of *tevhid* can only be understood by such an intellect. The people of *tevhid* are the people of silence because the person who knows with certainty that everything is from God has nothing left to object to. While a person at this level of understanding does see the multiplicity of, say, Aisha, Fatima, Ahmed, and Mehmed, at the same time they know that God alone is seen through them. This is why they don't get upset, angered, or bothered by anyone's words or actions. Let me share two anecdotes on this.

I mentioned this story earlier, where one day Abu Bakr was sitting with the Prophet. A man entered and started badmouthing Abu Bakr. Abu Bakr did not respond, and on seeing this, the Prophet smiled. Soon after, the same man started to swear at Abu Bakr. This time Abu Bakr defended himself, saying, "I am not like that; I am not as bad as you say." On hearing this, the Prophet stood up to leave. Abu Bakr was puzzled, and asked, "Why do you deprive us of your presence?" The Prophet said, "At first, when you saw the manifestation of Truth in the man, you were quiet, so angels surrounded you. By objecting, you objected to the Truth, so Satan has come right next to you. Since a prophet does not share the same place with Satan, I must leave."

Excessive protestations invite Satan, which takes a person further away from *tevhid*. Resorting to such behavior is wrong. One day Ahmed Rifa'i, who was known for his extreme humility, was invited to a fast-breaking dinner by one of his newly initiated disciples. They walked over to his house together and knocked on the door. His wife welcomed him and his children surrounded him. When the disciple saw his family, who he was very fond of, he forgot about Ahmed Rifa'i and closed the door. The man broke his fast with his family, had dinner, and was about to leave his house for the nightly prayer when he found Ahmed Rifa'i still waiting outside the door. Overcome with shame, he threw himself at Ahmed Rifa'i's feet and pleaded, "My teacher! Please forgive me!" Ahmed Rifa'i smiled and said, "My son, I know everything comes from God so I was not offended. Come, let's go and pray. We can eat later. Though I'm surprised at you. Did you think I was so unfaithful that I would leave (after you invited me)? Even dogs are as loyal as this. My son, do you think me to be at a station lower than a dog?" Ahmed Rifa'i is a great teacher.

You might raise a question here, "Is it that we are never supposed to object to people's mistakes? You said to object to someone's mistake is equivalent to objecting to God. So when someone commits an error such that it harms the nation or is an immoral crime that goes directly against divine law, are you saying that even then we shouldn't object?" Of course we should. Mansur Hallaj says, "To distinguish between faith and disbelief is disbelief because in *tevhid* even Moses and Pharaoh are the same. They are manifestations of different reflections of God's meaning. At the same time, to *not* distinguish between a believer and a disbeliever is also disbelief." In short, we have to intervene when an unbeliever commits a fault, but our objection has to conform to certain moral standards. We should warn without hurting anyone's feelings, and without angering them or pushing them further into disbelief. After giving three warnings to that person, if he still persists with his falsehood, we should abandon our effort to correct them and remember that this may not be the most opportune time to change their mind. I firmly believe that it is much more effective if we go about it in this way. People who are at the level of "spiritual teachers" should express their concerns with love. There is a Qur'anic verse that supports this point. God says to the Prophet, "By an act of mercy from God, you (Prophet) were gentle in your dealings with them – had you been harsh, or hard-hearted, they would have dispersed and left you – so pardon them and ask for forgiveness for them. Consult with them about matters; then, when you have decided on a course of action, put your trust in God: God loves those who put their trust in Him."[10]

In *Fihi Ma-Fihi*, Mevlana Rumi says, "If a student writes something for the first time, and his teacher says, 'O son, what ugly handwriting!' then that same student will never write anything again. A good teacher would praise the student and say, 'You have beautiful writing! But if you fix this letter, it will become even more beautiful.'" Over time, the writing of each letter improves,

---

10. Qur'an, *al-'Imran* (Family of 'Imran), (3:159). Tr. Haleem, *Qur'an*, p. 46.

and the student's overall handwriting becomes beautiful. Mevlana adds, "If you confront people about their ugliness, you will have no students left around you. Teach them by loving them, kissing them and appreciating them. Set an example yourself; train them as if you had made the mistakes. Soon you will see that they too will have a loving approach with you and, without realizing it, they will begin to struggle to correct their mistakes."

Over the last twenty years that I have been teaching, this is the approach I have adopted and I love it. I want to share a very simple but significant story. During my first year of teaching, I caught one of my students cheating during an exam. I used to help my students individually, even on exams. So his cheating despite all my help upset me greatly. "This is not how humans behave!" I had said. I was young and inexperienced. After this episode, I tried not to use such language. As I said, I was a young girl and I made a mistake. The child turned to me and replied, "You're an animal!" Obviously, I was thoroughly embarrassed in front of the entire class. I cried, and because *tevhid* had not manifested in me, I was upset for the student as well. I felt that I had disgraced myself. When I went home and consulted my family, different people gave me different advice. In the end I decided to take the matter in my own hands. The student was the kind of child that all teachers complained about. I called him to my office and said, "I love you so much, you don't have to love me in return, but you do have to pass this class because you have to respect my love for you. At least make an effort to get a D so I can pass you." He said nothing and continued with his cold and bullying ways. After a week had passed, he left school for some time. I was extremely concerned, and wanted to know whether he was ill or if it was something else, so I started to search for him. After a while, he suddenly showed up. He walked into class, placed the textbook in front of me, and in an aggressive tone said that he would be willing to take an oral exam. I asked him a question, he answered, and I said, "Okay, good, you can sit down now." He refused and told me to ask more questions. By the end, he had practically covered the entire book; clearly, he had memorized it! Eventually he became one of my best friends and is one of my most beloved students. I hope he is listening; he might remember this incident. He taught me something: "Sweet words can melt even the hard-hearted." There are very few things in the world that can't be solved with love. Sure, you might not be able to bring about a change in the Abu Jahls of this world, but love and kindness can do so much in the world.

Q: You said that a spiritual teacher uses love more than anything else to teach students. How would you describe the teaching style of spiritual guides?

A: A Perfected Human has reached the station of seeing God in all people. There is a famous *hadith* of the Prophet that states, "When needy persons extend their hands to you, the alms that you give them land in God's hand before reaching their hands." 'Abd al-Karim al-Jili explains this as follows: "When you get angry with someone and shout at them, your bitter words reach God first. So be ashamed and refrain from uttering such words." A Perfected Human who has attained this understanding of *tevhid* unfailingly deals with every human being as if they were dealing with God.

Scientists are aware that everything is made of water and that water turns to ice when it is cold. Yet, the essence of the ice doesn't change; it is the same water. Scientists also know that in different environments ice can form prisms that reflect light in a variety of colors. Similarly, a Perfected Human knows that the essence of everything is God, and he can see that all things solidify to varying degrees depending on the conditions of this world. Solidified matter then transforms into prisms that reflect color according to their different natures and dispositions. So a Perfected Human might say, "My beloved God! You manifest in such a violent manner, but also through such beautiful words." Perfected Humans embrace these manifestations of God with love instead of getting angry. They observe the manifestation of their Beloved through different mirrors. As a result, they never mistreat any other person. Kenan Rifa'i once said, "When I have to scold people whose spiritual development is my responsibility, I feel very sad when I get home because it is not my disposition to scold." However, sometimes we have to punish our children so that they grow up to become well-mannered and courteous.

Children are divine trusts that we have been given. At the end of our lives, God will ask us: "Did you try to teach them beautiful conduct and the best manners? Did you struggle in the way of this cause? Or were you lax about it? Or did you claim your children as your own and spoil them with excessive love?" We will be responsible for answering these questions.

As you know, the Prophet did not confront people about their faults. Even though he knew people's feelings and thoughts – and their secrets – he covered their faults and treated everybody with the utmost kindness. The following story illustrates this point: a woman came up to him one day and said, "O Messenger of God, please punish me. I have committed adultery," she pleaded. "No, you have not," the Prophet replied with a smile on his blessed face. The woman insisted that she had. "No, you have not," he said again. For a third time the woman repeated, "I have committed adultery." Only then did the Prophet ask if she had two witnesses. "Yes, I do," the woman replied. And only after her own pleading did the Prophet agree to deliver the punishment. We are the children of a Prophet who goes to great lengths to cover people's faults and forgive them. We are under the guidance of a friend (of God) who forgives people's mistakes. How can anyone forget the incredible story about 'Ali in which he was about to cut the head of a disbeliever with his sword? Just before doing so, the disbeliever spat on his face. 'Ali lowered his sword and said, "You insulted my *nefis*. I cannot kill anyone because of my *nefis*, as that would make me a murderer." On hearing this, the man threw himself at 'Ali's feet and embraced Islam, saying, "What a great teacher, what an exalted human you are!" Can we ever forget this?

Q: In fact, don't they cut the *nefis* with the sword of *hilm* (gentleness)?

A: Yes. A Perfected Human is the one who has erased all the excessiveness of their *nefis* with the sword of gentleness, softness, politeness, and love. There are Perfected Humans in whom the divine attribute of majesty prevails. However, the manifestation of this majesty reflects knowledge onto people's hearts; it does not hurt or upset them. This is why to see and know a Perfected Human is such a great blessing. May God grant this blessing to everyone.

On the night of the ascension, when the Prophet Muhammad requested God's mercy and forgiveness for his people, God replied, "All your wishes will be granted. You have seen Me in all people and loved Me in all people. You never got upset, and You have never despaired. Even when you were pelted by hundreds of stones in Ta'if[11] and were bleeding all over, you raised your hands and prayed to Me, 'O Lord, forgive these people for they don't

---

11. According to early Muslim history, this refers to an incident when Muhammad and his adopted son Zayd visited the town of Ta'if (south of Mecca) to invite

know me! Please make the offspring that come forth from them obey you.' You are the one who sees Me and knows Me in all things. For this reason I grant you all your wishes. Your people will always be of three types: those who rebel, those who obey, and those who yearn for their Lord like a thirsty man searching for water in a desert." At this point, God blesses us with great beauty and gives us glad tidings. He says, "I will bestow mercy and forgiveness for the rebellious people in your community. That is, I will force the rebellious servants to obey Me. I will grant paradise to those who obey. And to the thirsty, I will grant the happiness of seeing My eternal beauty." God also says, "The people of Moses and Jesus saw what they wanted to see according to their respective abilities. But your people (O Muhammad) are those who yearn for the spiritual realm, for the divine power that I have blessed to spirits, and for the path that reaches Me. In order to guide them on this Path, I have sent them, My friends, who are at the station of 'Ali and can set an example for them."

God shares with us this excellent news. We are immersed in this blessing. Our Exalted God, who calls even the rebellious people "My servants," who never gets angry – He is the most beautiful God. May He grant us servitude as an everlasting station.

The path is the illuminated heart. It means journeying towards oneself without one's self. It is to know and to find. We have to first leave ourselves, and then return to ourselves without our selves. In other words, we have to know our own reality. Eventually of course we will see our reality openly; at that time we will be in a state of unconditional *tevhid*. In order to find the road to *tevhid* we must first establish *tevhid* in ourselves. This means we must put an end to the unending battle between our *nefis* and spirit, which is a massive undertaking. Once we do this, that is, when we elevate ourselves to the level where we can be at peace with ourselves, then we aim for a higher level. In her book, *Follow Your Heart*, Susanna Tamaro[12] says, "For someone to successfully live up to an ideal, they must first end their own inner battles." So even for a person to say "I'm religious" or "well-mannered" or "a teacher," they must first settle the account with themselves. Unless a person has integrity and unity within, it's very difficult

---

its inhabitants to Islam. The elders of the city rejected Muhammad's message and instructed the children to throw stones at Muhammad to make him leave.

12. Susaana Tamaro is a contemporary Italian novelist.

for them to find God in others. Once they win the inner struggle, they are not affected by anything else. Moreover, when they are invited to the next world, they take their leave immediately.

For such people, the secret of the following *hadith* is evident: "Believers do not die; they move from one abode to another." What a beautiful secret this is; since they have overcome the struggle within, they cannot be offended or feel hurt. A person is offended when they are insecure and feel unloved. Can the person who has established a bond of trust and confidence with God ever feel unloved? The lovers of God are the closest friends to the people; they are consistently loyal. The extent of their loyalty is so deep that it is almost as if it compensates for all the unfaithful lovers we've had throughout our lives. They embrace and cover us. Life without them is so very difficult. How happy that person is who finds a perfect teacher who lives according to Muhammad's example. Teachers like this have reached the heights of beauty. They are the light of the Household of the Prophet and holders of the station of 'Ali, about whom Mevlana Rumi says, "He is Adam, Moses, and also Jesus. He is the gate to be passed through, because he says, 'I am the dot under the letter *Ba* (the letter 'B').'"[13] What does it mean to be the dot under the letter B? The letter B means body. *"Bismi'Llah al-rahman al-rahim* (In the Name of God, the most Beneficent, the most Merciful)" refers to the names and attributes of God who has clothed Himself with B. The Perfected Human possesses all these names and attributes. All the names and attributes when preceded by the letter B assume a bodily form. If that body distances itself from its excessive desires and annihilates itself, B becomes non-existent, leaving only the dot beneath it. Every name and attribute that can be attributed to God are manifest in that dot. That dot is 'Ali. It is the meaning and essence of everything. In a famous *hadith*, our Prophet says, "I am the city of knowledge, and 'Ali is its gate." And in sura 2:189 it is said, "... enter your houses from the gates." Why would God say such a thing? What this means is, "Enter the abode of the illuminated heart through the gate of 'Ali." Become enlightened with the light of 'Ali so that your heart is illuminated. We worry about breaking people's hearts. Is it possible to break the heart of a

---

13. The letter "b" in the Arabic script is transcribed as: "ب"

friend of God whose heart is illuminated? May God protect us from that.

Q: Was the command *"Kun* (Be)" given for these great people?

A: Yes. *Kun* means, "Be." *Kun* is made up of the Arabic letters *Kaf* and *nun*. *Kaf* represents all the names and attributes of God. His names and attributes have come together in a great teacher and it is not known whether this person exists or not, just like the legendary Mountain Qaf.[14] In order for the Perfected Human to be revealed, divine light must be projected onto them. When God's light is reflected on them, the command "Be" is given. The command "Be" is for people who possess all the names and attributes, like the prophecy that manifested for the Prophet Muhammad and his successors in the cave of Mount Hira. As for us, in reality we are not living beings; we are dead. We only live fleetingly when we establish a connection with such beautiful beings, and momentarily come alive and become "be."

Q: You said earlier that Perfected Human beings "are people who witness the Truth." Can you say more about these spiritual guides?

A: The Prophet's meaning can be thought of as *Qaf*. When we say, "I begin in the name of God," we begin with all the names and attributes that are manifested in humanity, and the most perfect of that humanity who is Muhammad. In saying this phrase, we also proclaim the name of 'Ali, who is the dot under the letter B. In other words, *"Bismi'Llah al-rahman al-rahim"* is to say, "I mention God, the Prophet, and the Perfected Human, all three at the same time." So it is a very important phrase. Christians have confused this three-fold station despite the beautiful teachings of Jesus; they consider these to be separate manifestations at three different stations. That is why they employ the term trinity. But these three stations should be understood as: the station of Divinity, the station of Prophethood, and the station of the Perfected Human. If *Qaf* – which is the great mountain that has never been seen but is known to all – is the Prophet Muhammad, then 'Ali is the possessor of all the names and attributes. He is the sovereign teacher who teaches us from his meaning. He is the

---

14. In modern Turkish, there is no distinction between *kaf* and the *qaf*.

Phoenix, which is the greatest and most beautiful bird ever that is said to have come from Mount *Qaf.*

The green color of the Phoenix points to the Prophet Khidr[15] (as well as the Khidr of the moment). It also communicates to us that the Phoenix leads to paradise, which is eternal, uninterrupted peace and (vision of God's) presence. Moreover, it explains the manifestation of the Real. What does the Real mean and what does it mean to be with the Real? It means the perfection of a human being. Humans have Preserved Tablets, which means their reality is predetermined. When that reality manifests, and when human beings reach (the meaning of) their Preserved Tablet, they become the Real. Mansur Hallaj's proclamation "I am the Truth!" actually means "I have reached (the meaning) of my preserved tablet, so the Real has become fully manifest through me!" He did not claim to be God. No. He said, "I am the Truth (*Hakk*), I am with the Truth." But people misunderstood and assumed that he was claiming to be God. They said, "How can you be God? Retract your words and save yourself!" they said. He replied, "I did not say I was God, I said I am the Truth. Whoever accused me of saying otherwise should take it back." He was a great saint.

> Q: Mevlana Rumi has said in the *Fihi Ma-Fihi,* "By proclaiming himself to be the Truth, Mansur Hallaj actually showed great humility because it represented the farthest most point of servitude." Could you please explain this?

A: Yes, Hallaj says, "I am a servant and I have annihilated myself." To this, Mevlana asks, "should he have said, 'I exist'? I and alongside of me, God exists." Mevlana explains that what Hallaj wanted to say was, "I have become annihilated and I have become one with God." He also says there are three ways of knowing the true meaning. "First, someone might know the meaning of there being one God, a prophet, and a Perfected Human. They know this intellectually, not because they have seen them. Second, a person might see that there is one God, a prophet, and a Perfected Human, and this person can see their meaning. Don't confuse this point. Seeing the meaning of the Prophet or 'Ali does not mean seeing their faces. Rather, seeing them means being able to find their reality in all people and things. When this witnessing reaches its highest level

---

15. The literal meaning of "Khidr" is the color green.

in a person and they become happy and content with everything, they begin to scream and shout about that which they witnessed. This was the station of Hallaj." Mevlana continues, "Then there are people like me who are lost in that meaning. They no longer exist as themselves. About whom will they speak, and to whom? They remain silent." Rumi was such a great saint.

Earlier you asked about the Perfected Human's station and if it is that of witnessing God and His Messenger in every thing and every place. Yes, it is such an exalted station that beauty emanates from it. A Perfected Human is in a state of non-existence; the extent of their humility reminds us of the dialogue between God and His Messenger on the night of the ascension. The Prophet said, "O Master, I am a servant! Please forgive the sins of this sinner!" God answered, "You are not a sinning servant, O Muhammad." Didn't the Prophet know that he was not a sinner? Yet, he knew very well that the path of gaining nearness to God is through the stations of servitude and nothingness. God is the Absolute Sovereign. If He pleases, He can change anything at any given moment. The Prophet knew this, and in another *hadith* he said, "O people, it is not certain that I will enter paradise. I have done many good deeds. But good deeds alone do not take people to paradise. Only one thing will take a person to paradise and to God's meaning, and that is God's blessing and generosity. I am the one who is most fearful that God's blessing and generosity will be cut off." Good deeds can only carry us as far as the Garden of Nai'm. The Garden of Nai'm is a garden inhabited by beautiful men and women, and with rivers of honey and many palaces. The servants, who chose to forgive others even when they had the power to punish, inhabit the uppermost palaces of this garden. They did this because they recognized God in everything. But such material beauty does not impress the real lovers of God. The only thing towards which they aspire is annihilation in their God. Only God's blessing and assistance makes it possible for the lover to be annihilated, to reach the garden of Beauty, and to become one with God. That is why our Prophet said, "I am the one who fears God most, and I am the ultimate servant, the absolute nothing, the absolute non-existing."

In reality, he is everything. In his character, he is God's He-ness. The Prophet's character is God's identity. God has become manifest through him. That is why the Prophet Muhammad is such a beautiful teacher. It is through him that all prayers are granted. At the same time, Perfected Humans are beloved to God. They ask nothing for themselves, but beseech their Beloved for others' needs. They are perfect lovers of God, and God grants them their prayers and wishes even though they don't want anything for themselves. When someone kneels in the presence of such a perfect guide, this should not be called "lunacy" or "craziness"; it communicates the extent of their neediness, as if they were saying, "Please cleanse me," which means, "Make me like you." This is not unlike when you go to a physicist or a chemistry teacher and ask them to teach you all the formulas they know, or the way to solve chemistry problems. Similarly we ask the spiritual guide, as if we were crying, "Help me please!" We take refuge in them since they are the ones who can resolve problems that relate to the body and the soul, as well as all kinds of worldly issues. And they are so great and so generous that they don't ask us for anything at all. They only show us by setting examples, just like God telling His Messenger, "Don't ask for any wage or reward in return, just give." They too just give and give and give more. They desire nothing in return. They are not affected by the state of our progress on the path to perfection. They are the people of *tevhid*, so they know that everyone has to act according to their Preserved Tablet. Being liberated in this way is what it means to be God's servant. However much a person aligns his actions to the words of his spiritual teacher – that is how much he protects himself from being enslaved by his *nefis* and reaches freedom in the real sense.

A disciple who has yet to overcome the inner battle with his soul hasn't experienced as much as a whiff of freedom, even though he might claim to be free. There is only one enemy for human beings, and it is their *nefis*. No harm comes to human beings from external enemies. If a person's faith is strong and resilient, then that person is free. Nothing can enslave or tie down the person with strong faith. What could possibly enslave a person like this? Some worldly event or incident? The mischief of others? My late teacher said in a poem, "From the perspective of *tevhid*; why complain so much about your *nefis*? It is only proper to appreciate the value of your *nefis*?" What my teacher means is, "Don't complain about your *nefis*, since through it you will become human." Your *nefis* will lead you to all kinds of blameworthy actions, but it is by resisting its temptations that you can progress. It will challenge you and you will struggle with it.

Just like Rumi's saying, "If there were no island, then there would be no battle." That is, if there were no land to be captured, then why would we fight? If that were the case, then we would be surrounded by Perfected Humans; they are free, they don't complain, and they are content with everything. The best example of this – of course everyone gives examples of their teacher! – was the time when my teacher Kenan Rifa'i's cough was getting worse and worse. The people around him begged him to ask God to take the cough away. They said, "O Master, why don't you pray that you be relieved of your cough so that you can continue to teach us?" He said, "O my children! How can I complain about a guest that has been sent by my dear God? If I complain about the guest to God, then it will complain about me too. I do my duty by waiting it out with respect so it can complete its duty as well." I can never forget this graceful response. Once we fully understand the fact that we don't see faults in others unless we possess those faults ourselves, then we can cover the eyes that see these faults. Seeing defects takes a person to very low stations.

I mentioned earlier the story about Shaykh Shibli. Shaykh Shibli said that there were three events from which he learnt important lessons: "A woman came to me. She was in a miserable state, totally disheveled. She said, 'O Shibli, my husband has left me! Do something to make him come back! I am miserable.' I said to her, 'O woman, pull yourself together! Fix your hair and regain your composure. Come back to me when you look decent and then proceed to make your request.' Shocked, she said to me, 'O Shibli! My love for my husband prevents me from seeing what condition I am in. You, who claim to be a lover of God, how is it that you notice the mistakes of others?' I was very ashamed and learnt an important lesson from this. The second event had to do with a child who was around ten years old. I lit a candle and haughtily asked the boy where the light of the candle comes from. He smiled, blew out the candle and answered, 'It comes from the same place where it has now gone.' I took many lessons from this, most importantly that we should never belittle or disrespect anyone. The third incident was the one which had the greatest impact on me; it involved a drunkard. He was staggering in the mud and looked like he was about to fall at any moment. I said to him, 'My son, you're going to fall down, and if you do you'll be rolling in mud! What is this condition of yours? Aren't you ashamed of yourself?' The drunkard replied, 'Oh forget it, Shibli! A bucket of water is all I need to wash myself clean. But you, you saw my fault. God never forgives those who see faults in others. God never washes things away for people of your spiritual stature. Shame on you!'"

A Perfected Human is a person of *tevhid* and they don't find fault in others. They see the beauty in everything and find beauty in everything. Let's end with an example from my teacher: He was sitting with his family one day when he noticed that a knife was lying on the dresser. He said to his family, "Put this knife away. If a child finds it, he might hurt himself. And just the same way, if we put away our bad habits, then we won't cut or hurt others." In *tevhid*, we see beauty in everything. May God grant us all that level *insha'Llah* (God willing).

Q: *Tevhid* means eternal presence, or being in the presence. What does being in the presence mean?

A: Being in the presence means to be in the presence of God. In other words, it means to be on the straight path and to be in paradise. Those who maintain this state are called "*hazret* (present)." It is said that those who cannot find paradise while in this world will not be able to find it in the next world. If the Hereafter is conceived in terms of its relation to the temporal world, then it is that which is hidden from the sun, whereas the temporal world is that which is visible because of the sun.

Shortly before she passed away, the great Sufi Samiha Ayverdi asked the people around her, "Why are you sad for me? I am just passing from this room to the other." This is the kind of understanding we want to reach. If we do, then death appears as pleasant and beautiful. When someone asked Kenan Rifa'i if death is coupled with pain, he said, "Recite Sura Joseph, and you will understand." The person read the Sura, and asked him again, "But which part of the chapter speaks about death?"

Zuleikha, the Egyptian's wife, tried in vain to explain the extent of Joseph's beauty to the women around her; rumors about her continued to spread. She decided to organize a dinner and to all her guests she gave sharp knives and some oranges to cut. When they started to peel and slice the oranges, she instructed Joseph to walk past them. On seeing him, they all sliced their fingers and hands. But they felt no pain. So how does this Qur'anic chapter address the question of pain in death? If someone has lived their entire life in the presence of God, then a beloved will be there to take them from the presence of God in this world to the next. If the person's beloved is a friend of God, then this friend will appear to them at the moment of death, just like Joseph, and they will not feel the pain of the spirit taking its leave from the soul. They will move from this life to the next, from one paradise to another, and from one state of presence to the next. Paradise means service. There is nothing that brings more peace than work. Action is life. Death means to stop being active. When God creates a human being, He bestows a great blessing, because it is impossible for anything that is annihilated in the eternity of God to know its Creator. A person can only recognize God when he sees His beauty in the other (distant self). When the human being receives God's blessing and comes to this world, he is given a warning, as stated in Sura al-Baqara (the Cow): in order to reach God, you must struggle, say your prayers, and be benevolent. Trusting in God is the path a person takes only after struggling and effort. These actions will lead a person to paradise.

There was a story about heaven and hell in one of the issues of Reader's Digest: The people of both heaven and hell were given spoons with very long handles. They were then asked to eat using these spoons. The inhabitants of hell tried to eat with these strange spoons and ended up spilling the food all over because eating and holding the handles at the same time proved to be an impossible task. The people of heaven, however, didn't have this problem because they were all feeding each other. An important maxim that my teacher Kenan Rifa'i would frequently say is: "Don't be a burden to others, be a friend to all." Don't oppress anyone, don't trouble anyone, and don't expect anything from anyone. Ahmed Rifa'i said, "Our path is founded on three key principles: to give to all those who want, to expect nothing from anyone, and to refrain from accumulating wealth." So let us give, let us be the ones who are always giving, and let us expect nothing from anyone. If we place ourselves on such a path of service, then there is always a paradise within us. People of tevhid are always in paradise because they see beauty in everything, divinity in everything. It is easier to explain this point with the help of a poem by my teacher:

Is God not absolute beauty?
Why should witnessing this be a sin?

126

Every beauty is proof of (His) power
Witnessing this beauty is worship

If God is absolute beauty, then why is it sinful to see the reflection of His beauty in human beings? Every kind of beauty is a proof of God's beauty. To witness it is no different from worship.

Nothing in this world is created in vain. Spiritual pleasure can be tasted when opposites come together. For instance, in a movie or in a play, if there were no villain that comes between two lovers, life would be monotonous. It would lack any excitement or thrill. We have seen many people who have no problems but who create problems. The most trivial of issues become serious trials for them. I have met women who have considered taking their own lives because their children received poor grades in school or because they had put on weight. All difficulties lead people to wistfully think, "We were so happy earlier, but we never realized this and failed to be grateful even for a single day!"

Friends of God don't like complaining. A dervish went to a doctor one day. The doctor asked him, "What's your complaint?" He said, "What kind of a question is that? I have no complaints!" But the person who accompanied him to the doctor's clinic warned the doctor, saying, "He is a dervish, so he never complains about anything. Ask him which part of his body is aching."

The person who knows his God doesn't like to say things like, "I'm ill." They know what great blessings illnesses are. It was reported in a *hadith*, "When a believer suffers malaria for a night, all the sins they committed for a year are forgiven." When a person understands the reasons behind all things, they thank God even for illnesses. Illness is a guest that God sends. Those who know this truth don't complain about the guest. They respect the guest instead. It is a wonderful thing to see the manifestations of the Truth in all places and in all things, and to witness the beauty of God. Let us witness God's kingdom even in the people who deny the Truth. Let us see the beauty in atheists and non-believers. Rumi says, "You need two opposing ideas to prove something." Without duality, it is impossible to establish *tevhid*. Somerset Maugham[16] said in one of his brilliant books, "The meaning of life is hidden in a Persian rug because the most beautiful and the ugliest of colors

---

16. William Somerset Maugham (d. 1965) was a British playwright, novelist and short story writer.

in the world have come together to produce an absolute master-piece!"

Q: Rumi says in *Fihi Ma-Fihi*, "God has created resources like grass, firewood, and cow manure. Although these are not very pleasant, they are great blessings for the owner of a Turkish bath (*hammam*). He uses these to heat up his bath and people benefit from it."

A: Imagine being in love with a beautiful person. Imagine that they are beautiful from head to toe. Their hair, skin, face...absolute beauty. Now, gouge out their eyes, chop off their hair and remove their intestines, and look at each of these separately. Suddenly you find yourself terrified and looking for a place to hide! So something that is extremely beautiful as a whole might become pretty ugly when looked at in its separate parts. We should train ourselves to see the whole all the time.

Q: Nothing is created in vain. Is it correct to say that if majesty and beauty were not united in a human being, then there would be no perfection?

A: In all of creation, it is only in the human being that there is both lordship and servitude. The human being carries the station of lordship, which the spirit represents, together with the station of servitude, which the *nefis* represents. God's perfection manifests in the human being both through His majesty and His beauty. Only those who understand *tevhid* are able to attain perfection. Ugliness and evil are degrees of beauty. For instance, the smell of a hyacinth is one of the most beautiful fragrances in the world. However, if you chemically extract the smell of a hyacinth, it will start to emit a putrid smell like that of manure. The difference between the smell of a hyacinth and manure is a difference of dose (chemically). Hence, beauty and ugliness are but differences of degrees on a scale. They are not different from each other in essence. Where they do differ is in the perspective of the viewer.

Q: In the *Mathnawi*, Mevlana Rumi says, "Unbelief (*kufr*) and religion (*din*) are one and the same thing, because religion means to give up unbelief."

A: Unbelief represents the body, and religion represents the unification of the *nefis* with the spirit in the body. It is as simple as that. Let me give you an example. Imagine a beautiful mansion on a large estate, but with one catch: the mansion is in need of a washroom. After a while a house without a washroom becomes hellish for anybody living there. On its own, a washroom might be seen as a dirty or even disgusting place, but in the mansion it serves a beautiful function. When we start seeing the whole, that is, if we direct ourselves towards *tevhid*, and become attentive to our own mistakes rather than constantly correcting those around us, and when we start loving all those around us, then we will develop the ability to discover the beauty that lies dormant in all of creation.

Let's talk about the different types of *tevhid*. The *tevhid* of the lay believers is to acknowledge God in all events and to see Him in everything. The *tevhid* of the elite is to not see the world at all; it is to be able to witness, in total amazement, the beauty of the Truth in all things with little effort. From the perspective of the elite, there is no such thing as a "cause" because the entire cosmos for them is an infinite manifestation of the Truth. The servant is the lover, and the Truth is the Beloved. In other words, God is sometimes, so to speak, "playful" with His servants.

There is a wonderful story in the oral tradition. It is said that back in the day, the rose used to be white. It was as white as snow. The nightingale was madly in love with the rose. You would always find the nightingale flying around the rose (similar to how we walk around God and the lovers of God). The rose feigned indifference, as it deliberately acted coy and playful with the nightingale. But the nightingale, eager to announce its love for the rose, came closer and closer. Eventually, the thorn of the rose, that is the thorn of life-events, pierced the nightingale's tiny heart, thus shedding the blood of its *nefis* on the roots and sap of the rose. So the blood of the nightingale changed the color of the rose to red, saturating it with the meaning of the Prophet. We too shed the blood of our *nefis* over God's rose of meaning. In other words, if we don't sacrifice our *nefis* in the presence of the Prophet's meaning, then we will not be able to achieve oneness with God, nor will we be able reflect His colors.

As for the *tevhid* of the elite, there is no such thing as attaining oneness with the Truth. "God was, and there was nothing alongside Him." That is, absolute unicity. God directed the Prophet to the paradigmatic model of Abraham because it was the model for this stage of *tevhid*. Nimrod threw Abraham into the fire and the fire transformed into a rose garden due to Abraham's contentment and submission. In other words, the fire turned into the meaning of the Prophet. Khalil (friend) [17] became Habib (beloved)[18] in that fire. Gabriel, or the intellect of Abraham, came to him and said, "I am here to help you seek God's help." Abraham replied, "No, I have no need of your help. My God knows my situation. I am in my ascension and have left behind my intellect. I have reached that Exalted King's presence. I am one with Him."

> Q: In sura *al-Ahqaf* (the Sand Dunes) it is said, "For those who say, 'Our lord is God,' and then follow the straight path, there is no fear, nor shall they grieve."[19] Are the people of *tevhid* the people who are committed to the Straight Path?

A: Being committed to the Straight Path means to purify oneself of all wants and desires other than God. In addition, of course, our relationship with people must be beautiful because it is for God that we serve humanity. We have to see the Truth in all of creation when we walk on this path and all our actions must be directed towards pleasing God through our service. This is to be like 'Umar, who occupies the station of *al-Samad* (the Eternal). The station of "*Allah al-Samad* (God the eternal)" in sura *Ikhlas* (Purity) is the manifestation of attributes in 'Umar. Because 'Umar saw nothing but God in all things, he was only responsible to God. He sought perfection and always acted with justice. 'Uthman represents "*lam yalid wa lam yulad* (He begot no one nor was He begotten)." He valued the station of God's incomparability (*tenzih*). 'Uthman is the exemplar of the attribute of proper conduct (*edep*). He was a beautiful human being, always occupied with his God as if he had no children and no parents. 'Ali, though, possesses in him the manifestation of the Essence. He is "*wa lam yakun lahu kufuwan ahad* (No one is comparable to Him)." Just like in the verse, "When you threw, it wasn't you who threw, but God,"[20] the Truth became manifest in him. If a person is committed to this path, *tevhid* becomes very easy. Action is also the manifestation of this meaning. It means to show the knowledge you learned for the sake of God through your state and comportment. Actually, knowledge is the Qur'an, and action is the Prophet Muhammad. The

---

17. The epithet by which Abraham was known, as the friend of God.
18. One of the epithets by which Muhammad was known, as the beloved of God.
19. Qur'an, *al-Ahqaf* (the Sand Dunes), (46:13). Tr. Haleem, *Qur'an*, p. 328.
20. Qur'an, *al-Anfal* (Battle Gains), (8:17).

two are actually one. The knowledge that we need to trust in is the Qur'an. The actions, personality, and power that we need to trust in are those of the Prophet Muhammad. If we act according to this, we too will reach the presence of God. Ultimately, a person reaches the stage where their relative being is consumed in God's being.

It is like Aziz Mahmood Hudai,[21] who said:

People of the world are in the world,
People of the Hereafter are in the next world,
All of them are after something
What I am after is my God

God gives the glad tidings that people who have found this path will have no fear nor will they grieve. When a person unites everybody and everything, there is no fear and grief left. Let me explain this with an example. One day, Jesus took refuge in a cave of jackals and said, "Let me take refuge from the rain and stay here for a while." At that moment, he received an order from God: "O Jesus, leave the jackal's cave at once. Your presence has made its babies uncomfortable." Jesus cried, "O Lord! The jackal has a home to take refuge in this world, but Jesus the son of Mary has neither a home, nor a place, nor a refuge!" Regarding this, Rumi says, "O Jesus! You have such a One Who has thrown you out from the house. Although you have no home, it is due to the blessing of the One Who has thrown you out and the honor of having such a station that you are asked to leave. This is worth hundreds of thousands of heavens and earths, worlds and next worlds, divine thrones and seats, even surpassing them in value. Why have fear?"

If a person who is at a similarly sublime station gets fired from his or her job, it is as if they were cast out of the cave. They should know that God would protect and provide for them if they lived a righteous and lawful life. When this is understood, who and what will we fear? Can anyone be even slightly fearful of what awaits him or her in the future? How can they worry about tomorrow when they are certain of their God and have reached the station of the trustworthy?

Some companions asked the Messenger of God one day, "What was there before the creation of the cosmos?" He answered, "God, and there was nothing alongside Him." They asked Junayd Baghdadi

21. Aziz Mahmud Hudai (d. 1628 CE) was a famous Sufi saint of the Ottoman Empire, founder of the Jelveti Sufi order.

to expand on this saying of the Messenger. He said, "It is still so." Nothing has changed ever since. All the people that we see are imaginary. God exists, and nothing exists with Him. When God's light appeared in non-existence, the physical realm came into being. Abu Madyan Maghribi[22] once said, "Is what is seen You or I? Please forgive me, for I am on the verge of dualism. My body is from You, and Your manifestation is through me. If it were not for You, I would not exist. Yet if it were not for me, You would not be manifest." Thus, all of creation is a veil, created in order for Him to manifest Himself. When this reality becomes evident, there is no reason to be upset.

Another meaning of *tevhid* is to not associate any partners with God. The *tevhid* of the spiritually mature means: to see nothing in the universe besides God, to know that every encounter and interaction is only with God, and to acknowledge with certainty that God is with them at all times. Prayer is a practice that represents *tevhid*.

Mevlana Rumi notes, "Prayers performed by lay believers are the five prescribed prayers (at specified times of the day). But the prayer of the lovers is unceasing." Those who are in a state of constant prayer are the most unwavering on this path. What does "constant prayer" mean? It is to establish a connection with God through our hearts, and to prostrate before Him in servitude. When we are afflicted with difficulty, to prostrate and accept the trial with contentment and without objection; to do this is to be at the highest station. This station of contentment leads a person to *tevhid*. One day they told my teacher, "May God be pleased with you," and he replied, "Let me be pleased with Him first." Amazed, they inquired, "What do you mean by that?" and he replied, "Unless I am pleased with my God, He won't be pleased with me. Let me receive all that is from Him with contentment and submission, and then He will be pleased with me as well." This is the essence of the matter. When we understand what it means to be thankful for everything and to see the inherent beauty in all things, then God will be pleased with us. When a person tastes the pleasure of pleasing God, then everything becomes beautiful. In order to please God, we must be people of service. We need to work for people. People of service are the people of presence; they are envel-

22. Abu Madyan Maghribi (d. 1198 CE) was a famous Andalusian mystic and Sufi master.

oped and illuminated with divine light. This explains why beautiful people have luminous faces. Their faces are full of love, enthusiasm, happiness, and excitement. Their love is endless. They never get old. They treat one another with love, and speak words of love and compassion to each other. Why would anything anger or upset such people of *tevhid*?

Somebody asked Jesus, "What are you most afraid of?" He replied, "God's wrath." The person pressed further, "How do we protect ourselves from His wrath?" Jesus replied, "By overcoming our wrath."

Be angry? At what? And at whom? One of my teachers told me, "When you get angry while driving, imagine that the person who angered you is a friend of God and withhold your anger." What opens the gates of paradise is only *tevhid*. And to attain *tevhid*, we have to be present in the moment and avail it fully. We have to take it from *Hayy* (the Everliving) to *Hu* (He). The moment comes with *Hayy* and flows to *Hu*. In other words, we come alive in every moment with *Hayy*. And if we are living righteously without any apprehensions about tomorrow, and if we are serving humanity and pleasing God, then the breaths that we take in and out go to *Hu* – their real master. We should always remember that the name of the gatekeeper of paradise is Ridwan, meaning the most exalted from among the contented ones. We should also bear in mind that the name of the gatekeeper of hell is Malik, meaning king. So worshipping worldly possessions leads a person to hell. Now you'll ask if it is wrong to possess any worldly belongings, like houses or cars. Of course to possess these things is not wrong; my point is that we should not worship them.

We should not claim worldly possessions as our own lest we be shattered when they are gone. People's efforts and resolve are not enough to take them to paradise. For this, a person has to receive God's blessing and kindness. Believers should apply their hearts with firm resolve and channel their intellect with wisdom, so that all these receptacles of knowledge bring them closer to God. Believers should open their hearts to the divine light, which is His grace and benevolence. They must establish a connection with God so that they can receive God's grace and divine light from His meaning. They must direct their intellect towards wisdom, at which point their intellect can see God in all things and they can attain *tevhid*. Knowledge is only that which takes a person to God.

If scientific disciplines bless human beings with the meaning of God, then they can be called sciences. Otherwise, they are useless. Today, there are people with three university degrees but they are unhappy and commit suicide and set bad examples for those around them.

> Q: They have opened the gates of Paradise, so hasten with determination
> The gatekeepers are always summoning the faithful,

> May God's grace and blessings be with you,
> O people of faith and piety, "Enter it and abide forever therein"[23]

> If the faith of the faithful is unconditional,
> then they will always refrain from sin and perform good deeds

> For the intoxicated, the affairs of the world are a mirror of God, while paradise for them is servitude. In them is the reflection of divine names.

> When their faith reaches certainty, they shed their ego, adorn the attributes of the Truth, and surrender ownership over their actions

> They manifest God's attributes, and enter the paradise of the heart, forever quenched through purity and sincerity in the mirror of divine signs

> When the faith of the faithful attains intoxication, all veils are then lifted and not a single attribute from the realm of multiplicity remains

> In the condition of perplexity there is no trace of the color of their self,
> Their paradise is the spirit, and it drinks in union with God's essence

> They immediately shun the falsity of their existence,
> Union with God erases any transcript of their name or trace

> Awestruck by God's beauty, they lose all volition,
> Ecstatic from head to toe, intoxicated, they enter perplexity upon perplexity

---

23. Qur'an, *al-Zumar* (The Throngs), (39:73).

Paradise of God's Essence is for those whose faith experiences
    certainty,
Overcoming duality, their faith travels to the Throne of Eternity

Sipping the joy of union, they arrive at their origin,
They are now one with the origin, joining in the love for unity

Those who guard their hearts are taken to paradise every
    moment in safety
The keepers of paradise say, "Enter it and abide forever therein"

This paradise, this piety, this faith,
May God always grant these to Ken'an in both worlds[24]

A: My teacher says, "They opened the gate of paradise. Who
opened it? The Perfected Human beings. They have opened the
doors, so let's hurry up." The keepers of the treasures are speaking
to the faithful here. Those who open the gates of paradise are the
Perfected Humans. And for whom do they open these gates? Let's
answer this. In sura *Yasin*, God says, "You can warn only those who
will follow the Qur'an and hold the Merciful One in awe, though
they cannot see Him: give such people the glad news of forgiveness and a noble reward."[25] So who are the ones who follow the
message? Those who obey divine orders and are in awe of the All-
Merciful, Unseen God. Although you have opened the door, you
can only impact people of this class. The unseen refers to the wisdom that we are temporarily unable to see, even though it is real.
To be in awe of God is to tremble with reverential fear when we feel
and witness the unseen of God. It is to fall in love with His beauty
and fear His majesty and to feel compelled to always obey His
commands. God says, "I have thrown open the gates of paradise
for people who can find contentment in my beauty and majesty. I
am giving away My treasures, so come running!" He adds, "But in
order to enter, you must first attain the station of contentment."
May God's blessing and peace be on you.

    Sura *al-Zumar* (the Throngs) speaks to the people of piety
(*takva*: doing what God has commanded and refraining from what
He has forbidden) and the people of faith (*iman*: recognizing God
in everybody and everything): "Enter paradise to abide therein

---

24. From the poem, "Degrees of Faith" by Kenan Rifa'i. See Kenan Rifa'i, *Ilahiyat-ı
Ken'an*, ed. Yusuf Ömürlü and Dinçer Dalkılıç, (Istanbul, 1988), p. 173.

25. Qur'an, *Ya Sin*, (36:11). Tr. Haleem, *Qur'an*, p. 281.

forever."[26] Here, my teacher says, "If you reach this station, you will enter paradise while still in this world and shall abide therein forever." If a believer's faith is based on imitation, that is, if he is only at the level of Şeriat (legal rulings), then that believer is a person of piety. While he performs righteous deeds, he continues to yearn for paradise and fear hell. So his peace does get interrupted from time to time. His is the station of certainty of knowledge (ilm-el yakin Ar. 'ilm al-yaqin). While his faith is good, it is still wanting. If he becomes intoxicated by the mirror of actions and comes to know what paradise is, that is, if he grasps that whatever he does is from God and the actions of others are from God, then his servitude becomes his paradise. He says, "I exist, and You also exist, but whatever I do, I do it by Your command." Because he acknowledges his nothingness he is in paradise. My teacher says that he has reached the station of seeing with God's names. If he progresses further and increases his faith, then he leaves behind the qualities of the nefis and starts to use his faculties only for God. Put differently, the manifestation of his actions enables an enlightened state such that he moves from being a human animal (beşer; Ar. bashar) to a human being (insan). Life-events are the mirrors that teach him to act with purity and sincerity. What is sincerity (ihlas; Ar. ikhlas)? It is to know that nothing you do is yours; rather, everything belongs to God alone. Hence, it is to know this and do everything without fear. The highest station of sincerity is that of 'Ali. Let me give you an example. When the Prophet asked his companions, "Who will take my place in the bed? I have received the order to leave," 'Ali immediately volunteered, saying, "I will take your place." Anyone could have said, "I will!" But 'Ali put the blanket over his head, fell into a deep sleep and started snoring. This is what sincerity means. When a person acts with sincerity, he possesses genuine peace in the presence of God.

Faith that is based on witnessing is an even greater station. A person at this station no longer acts in contradictory ways, nor does he possess qualities that are in opposition. Tevhid is established in him. Envy turns to admiration for him. Separation is removed from the heart, and is replaced by tevhid. His qualities are perfected. Tevhid manifests. His paradise is the paradise of the spirit. In other words, his spirit gains full control of the body. This

---

26. Quran, al-Zumar (the Throngs), (39:73).

individual becomes a true human being. He renounces his intellect at that majestic door, and the confirmation from God can be heard, "O *Ya Sin*, come!" When the Prophet surpassed the Lote Tree of the Farthest Point, this is also how he was summoned: "Come O *Ya Sin*! Come O Perfected Human! O Muhammad, you have become a Real Human Being." He was united with God's essence and nourished by it, such that he was in a state of continuous intoxication. The Prophet is protected from his temporary body; he is joined with God, though without any outer or apparent signs. Through God's grace he no longer has a will of his own. He is in a state of perplexity. He is not awestruck, rather in a state of perplexity.

We talked about how it was important for a person to maintain his awe of God in the face of God's beauty and majesty. We said that to be in this state meant to embrace both beauty and majesty. But it also means that in this state, God's beauty and majesty are seen as different from each other, whereas in the state of perplexity, there is no beauty or majesty left. They become one, and leave the servant in a state of utter bewilderment. Bewilderment in *tevhid* makes perplexity its primary principle (*mezhep* Ar. *madhab*). The paradise of the person at the station of certainty of truth (*hakk el-yakin*) is the Paradise of God's Essence. Their spirit has reunited with the Essence, as it has been said in the *hadith*, "...I become the hearing with which he hears and the seeing with which he sees, and the tongue with which he speaks..." We find such people speaking with God and seeing with God. They journey with God, having now been joined with the One. They have surpassed the stage of unity and have reunited with their origin. Having established *tevhid*, they have surpassed oneness and returned to multiplicity. The illuminated heart is in *tevhid* while the state of their being is multiplicity (*tefrik*). Through the happiness of unity, they reach their origin; together, with their origin, they experience the love of union. Those who God protects from their *nefis* are led to paradise in every moment, and they abide there forever on account of their perseverance in beautiful conduct. My teacher humbly says in the last quatrain, "May God allow us to reach that paradise and may He never cause us to leave it."

You said "my master" (*effendim*) when referring to Kenan Rifa'i. Some people may misunderstand why you used that term for him. He is a saint who has endowed us with perfect conduct and made us respected human beings. Since he had purified himself of the

vices of his *nefis*, he was able to lead us on the path to real freedom from our souls. In this way, he opened up the road to genuine happiness for us. It is under his guidance that we have become
respected human beings. He was a great master who taught us how
to become well-mannered servants. This is why there is absolutely
nothing wrong with you calling him "my master." May God allow
everyone to understand this.

Chapter Five:
Prayer (*Namaz*)

Q: We have talked about love, patience, destiny, etc. and said how important these qualities are in our lives. Let us now turn to worship, which is obligatory for us as human beings and for our lives as a whole. The greatest form of worship is prayer. We'll try to describe its inner and outer aspects. Worship covers many aspects of our lives. It wouldn't be wrong to say, would it, that our entire life can be viewed as an act of worship? To begin, what is worship in its apparent sense? It is repeatedly explained in the Qur'an and frequently mentioned by Perfected Humans. If we were to speak about worship in its general meaning though, where would we begin?

A: I'd like to begin with a story about a knower of God (*arif bi'Llah*) who was listening to a sermon in a mosque. The Imam (prayer leader) of the mosque was speaking at length about hell. When the Imam began to explain in great detail how people would burn because of their sins, the *arif* was saddened and said, "O Imam! God is not going to ask us what you say He will. He is going to ask us only one thing, 'My servant, I was with you all your life; who were you with?'" Worship encompasses all the states and actions that will allow us to say, "I was with You!" A person's desire to be with their Beloved is what brings them to this level.

But outer actions are also called worship. Mevlana Rumi says, "Piety (*takva*)" – that is, the fire of worship – "has burned the world and everything except God. Then the lightning of God's self-disclosure (*tecelli*) struck, eventually burning piety itself." This is a very important point. What does it mean to say that everything begins with piety? Three levels of piety are spoken of here. In the first degree of piety, what matters is to obey God's prohibitions. When a person falls in love, how easily they renounce so many things for their beloved, even the things they like, yes? What if this love is the love of God that has prevailed in a person? So performing prayer outwardly keeps a person away from all things declared unlawful by God. And if a person refrains from unlawful things, their love will increase. The more the love increases, the more a person will distance herself from everything except God. It is important to be clear, that this is not to say we should all become hermits. No. A person must see all beauty, and find God in all that beauty, as captured in the poem by my teacher Kenan Rifa'i:

Is Allah not Absolute Beauty?
Why should witnessing this be a sin?
All beauty is proof of (His) power
To witness this beauty is worship

When people arrive at this stage, they renounce everything that takes them away from God, as if these things never existed. The self-disclosure of God burns the human being. Due to the tremendous intensity of this disclosure, there is nothing left to exist, not even the form. That is, the human is completely annihilated in God's Essence. It is this state that Mevlana Rumi refers to as "drowning." Rumi says in *Fihi Ma-Fihi*, "Dip a bee in a honey barrel. The bee will no longer be able to move on its own. All its movement will be with the honey. What moves is the honey, not the bee. Outwardly there is still a bee, and the weight of the honey has increased as much as the weight of the bee. But what is moving is the honey." The human being arrives at this state. God becomes the speech with which he speaks and the sight with which he sees; God becomes the doer. But if you pay attention, you will note that to arrive at this state, Mevlana began with servitude; he began with non-existence. Prayer is to say, "I love You, God" through different human actions and states. Underlying these actions are several types of worship, including sacrifice, unity, ascension, alms, purity of state (*halin zekatı*), and purity of time (*vaktin zekatı*). This is why prayer is the most important worship.

In the same way that a person dresses up before going to meet their sweetheart, people purify themselves before prayer. A believer enters the presence of God – their most beloved – in ritual purity, having made the ablution. This is not just a formality; it is extremely important. Even though a person may have showered and may be physically clean, if they plan to pray, they must go back and perform ablution with the intention of attaining ritual purity. The outer meaning of ablution is to purify the self of all physical impurities. But it has many inner meanings. What are these? To purify and cleanse our bodily limbs of their sins is an act of beauty and benevolence. The more that people serve humanity and sacrifice what they have – including their possessions, their health, and their state – the more their bodies are purified of their sins. The soul is purified when a person adopts the conduct of God, comprehends the meaning of the Prophet, lives according to the Prophet's conduct, and is in a constant state of repentance. As for the purification of the secret, it is contingent on the relinquishing of all that is other than God. The person who performs ablution goes through all of these steps. The *arif* reminds him of what is required by saying the following words:

> While washing our hands, we ask, "My Lord, please help to make our hands an instrument for good deeds!"

> While washing our mouth, we say, "My Lord, please help us drink the wine of Kawthar!"

> While washing our nose, we say, "My Lord, please make me smell the heavenly fragrances!"

> While washing our face, we say, "My Lord, please illuminate my face just like you have illuminated the faces of Your beloveds."

> While washing our right arm, we say, "My Lord, please make me one of the repentant ones."

> While washing our left arm, we say, "My Lord, please make me of those who repent!"

> While wiping our head, we say, "My Lord, make me among those of Your servants for whom there is neither fear nor grief!"

> While washing our feet, we say, "My Lord, on that day when the feet of the hypocrites are made to slide, keep my feet firm on the Straight Path!"

> And then we recite, "*Amantu bi'Llahi* (I believe in God)."

Q: Since we are going for a meeting and have an appointment with our Beloved, we must go in the most beautiful form, and we must prepare each of our limbs for the expression of this intention.

A: We remind ourselves of this, which means that we purify our body, soul, and mind.

Q: Ablution functions like a filter, doesn't it?

A: Very true. There is a saying that "during prayer, a believer should not recite the Qur'an too loudly nor too softly," in order to remain alert and aware. As Ibn 'Arabi says, "Begin your worship as a servant so that God can become manifest through you. God's manifestation does not occur unless you begin as a servant." That's why we begin our prayer as servants. This is what it's all about.

We might ask, what is the purpose of prayer? As you know, God says in sura al-Kawthar (Abundance), "We have granted Kawthar to you." The Kawthar that is given here is to remind us that we have been granted a blessing. As noted by Junayd Baghdadi, "The color of the water depends on the vessel carrying it." Similarly, our perception of the blessing also depends on the vessel. Which blessing, though? "We have granted to you the drunkenness and spiritual pleasure of the wine of Kawthar that comes forth from the Prophet," and "We have bestowed upon you meaning from Our Meaning; We enlightened your spirit by way of the illuminated heart. We established your connection with Allah." There is so much to be understood from this. In sum, "We have given you love." So what should you do to remember this and be thankful for it? "Prostrate and sacrifice."

Let us turn to the phrase "So prostrate and sacrifice." The purpose of prostration is to rise to the level of being nothing during prayer, which you began as "I." This is because God takes hold of us by our foreheads during prostration. If a person comprehends their nothingness, then God connects with their intellect, which knows its nothingness.

There is also sacrifice in prayer, isn't there? So, prayer and sacrifice are mentioned side by side, meaning that these two should be together. The main purpose of sacrifice is to sacrifice the nefis. Just as we have to establish prayer in its outer form in order to understand its inner meanings, we must also establish sacrifice in its outer form by sacrificing an animal before we sacrifice our *nefis*. The inner meaning of sacrificing the *nefis* is to sacrifice the desires of *nefis*. If you don't do this, you'll become "cut off (*abtar*)," God forbid; your offspring, your meaning, and everything will be cut off. There are many lessons to be drawn from this. First, we understand the following: that we should "do this and keep doing this so that we can penetrate the real meaning." The continuity of *Kawthar* is sustained through prayer, the meaning of which is to sacrifice the pleasures of your *nefis*. These are intertwined. So what does it mean to sacrifice the pleasures of your *nefis*? Let's expand on this a little.

God says, "One edge of your two-edged sword (the sword of 'Ali) is opposition."

It means you will face all kinds of obstacles in your life. Your ideas will be challenged, but you won't allow these to detain you on your path. You will struggle, and there will be people who don't love you and will oppose you. All this opposition will enable you to cut the desires of your *nefis*. This is one edge of the sword. The second edge is the act of striving. If you continue to strive like the Prophet did, despite all these obstacles, this two-edged sword will cut the desires of your *nefis* and you will reach a state where your flesh will become beneficial to you. This is just like the sacrificed animal's meat, the portion that we bring home; in this case, it is in the home of your body that the meaning of God manifests. This makes both you and those around you peaceful, and you become beneficial for those around you that are spiritually poor.

It is stated in sura *Hajj* that in this sacrifice, three things play a role: the sword of Şeriat, the right conduct of Sufism (that is, the ability to see the Truth everywhere), and the great beauty that emerges when you cut off the desires of the *nefis*. All three of these allow you to serve as an example.

Q: This helps us to better understand the meaning of 'Ali, doesn't it? He did not say "I am divorced from the world" without any purpose.

A: 'Ali's sword is a sword of gentleness as well as chivalry. 'Ali is God's lion, and he did fight in battles; but, as you know, when his enemy spat in his face, he threw away his sword. He is this kind of lion of God. The man who spat in his face became Muslim and asked, "Why didn't you cut my head O 'Ali?" 'Ali said, "I cut the desires of your *nefis* with my sword of gentleness and knowledge, and look what a state you attained!" That is why this double-edged sword is the sword that sacrifices the *nefis*, and ʿAli is its meaning. The Prophet said, "I am the city of knowledge, and ʿAli is its gate." ʿAli is also the door of the Kaʿba. In order for us to find God in our hearts, we need ʿAli; that is, we need a friend of God (*veli*). Prayer contains sacrifice (*kurban*), hajj (*hac*), ascension (*mirac*), alms (*zekat*), and unity (*tevhid*).

Let us now turn to presence (*huzur*). As you know, prayer has two aspects. The first is to pray in peace. To pray in peace means praying in the presence, that is, feeling the self to be in the presence of God. That is the only way a person can elevate him or herself to God's presence. But we don't see God openly! So we can do two things: since we have been promised that "ascension (*mirac*) is in the prayer,"[1] and that "we will see (God)," but we are not yet at the level of seeing or witnessing God, so we begin the prayer as "I" and focus on the fact that God sees us. That's how we can rise to the presence.

Abu Saʿid al-Kharraz (d. 286/899), one of the greatest early Sufis, was asked, "How do you begin your prayers?" He answered, "As if you were standing in the presence of God on the Day of Judgment, when there will be no intermediary between you and Him. He will look at you and ask, and you will answer Him. You should stand there knowing that you are in the presence of the Sultan of sultans, and this experience will give you endless joy."

The second aspect of prayer is to find peace and presence by obeying the divine command in the verse, "Prostrate before Adam."[2] Standing in front of the Present One (*Hazret*) allows a person to be present, comfortable, and content.

In so many verses in the Qur'an, prayer is termed "*salat*." *Salat* means separation from your home. It refers to our separation from the pre-eternal realm. Prayer becomes obligatory at age seven, and jurists maintain that this is so because a person who has been away from their real home for seven years gets homesick. Since worship reminds us where we have come from and helps us reach presence, it (worship) is extremely important. When we begin the prayer with an Imam, we say "*Allahu Akbar* (God is Great)." The meaning of this

---

1. Refers to a saying of the Prophet Muhammad, which states, "Prayer is the ascension of the believer."
2. Qur'an, *al-Baqara* (The Cow), (2:34).

is, "O God, I sacrifice my *nefis* in Your Presence." In order to do this, we hold up our hands with our palms facing forward, meaning that we renounce both this world and the next. There is only me – the servant – and God. This is such an important state; it is the state of Muhammad. Prayer begins with the station of duality, which is also a station of nearness. Praise is offered for the Greatest One. The person continues to pray with the manifestation of the name of Muhammad at the level of nearness. During prostration, the truth of the Prophet emerges (*Ahmad*). It emerges with the manifestation of the name *Mahmud* (praised one) as well. And finally, the praying servant experiences the joy of being chosen (*Mustafa*).[3] Prayer is the only worship in which the person enters as "I," and if the prayer is completed with meaning, they leave as "the chosen servant;" the servant reaches the station of nearness to God.

When we are about to slaughter our sacrificial animal, we again say "*Allahu Akbar* (God is Great)"; that is, we say the same words as when we sacrificed the *nefis* that was worthy of being killed. At that moment, the body is Ishmael, and the spirit like *Khalil* (Friend).[4] The spirit says "*Allahu Akbar*" to cut this body from its desires and ambitions. Then the body is purged of its lusts and carnal inclinations, and "*Subhanaka* (Glory be to you)" is recited. *Subhanaka* means that God transcends everything.

Q: We always mention our dear Prophet. It is, of course, impossible not to mention him all the time. He is the crown on our heads and the light of our eyes. And there is prayer, which is the light of his blessed eyes. Prophetic sayings about prayer are as many as Qur'anic verses about prayer. The first five verses of sura *al-Baqara* (The Cow) list the qualities of those who have faith. It says, "Those who have faith in the Unseen establish their prayers and give of the provisions." These verses make it clear that one of the main conditions of being faithful is prayer. We'll come to the other two as well, but let us, if you like, start with prayer, the light (*nur*) of our Prophet's eyes...

A: As you know, according to a *hadith*, the Prophet said, "I have been made to love three things from your world; women, fragrance, and the light of my eyes, prayer." Grammatically, between two feminine

---

3. The names Ahmad, Mahmud and Mustafa are all epithets of the Prophet Muhammad.

4. *Khalil* or "Friend (of God)" is another title or name for Abraham.

nouns is the masculine noun "fragrance." This order does not follow a conventional Arabic sentence structure. Hence, this grammatical order demonstrates that the Prophet was made to say this sentence by God in a state of absolute servitude, and that God willed him to say this sentence. Its inconsistency with other *hadith* – which illustrate his perfect use of Arabic grammar in speech – demonstrates this point. Now if you ask if this makes it any different from other sayings of the Prophet, of course it doesn't. But the grammatical order does highlight the fact that the Prophet's statement is a sign of faith in the unseen. In a way, creation is being explained here. According to Ibn 'Arabi, God created man first by blowing His own spirit into him, and then He created woman, who is a part, and partner, and the other half. The Arabic order explains God's existence and the creation of men and women. With the feminine, what is spoken of is the *nefis*. This same explanation can be frequently found in religious literature. *Nefis* is the most important part of the body since it possesses the power to reach the station of the spirit and to mold a person's character. When we manage to cleanse the *nefis* of its worldly desires, it transforms into the spirit. Whereas previously it was called *nefis*, now, praise be to God, it is spirit. That's why the *nefis* is such a sublime station. It is the station of Zuleikha.[5]

> Why complain about the *nefis*? Is it fair to consider it unworthy?
> It is a great blessing for you from the Sublime God.
>
> It is your companion; don't look at it with disdain; use it
>   rightfully.
> By knowing your *nefis*, you can know God and the taste of union.
>
> Can you arrive at your destination without the *nefis*?
> At the end of your life, it (*nefis*) won't let you suffer separation.
>
> Do not separate it (*nefis*) from knowledge and good conduct.
> Appreciate its value, serve it as best as you can, and don't let
>   it complain about you.
>
> My words will have meaning only after spiritual training.
> Benevolence for Ken'an! By curbing your *nefis*, you become a
>   human being.[6]

---

5. See Glossary.

6. Ken'an Rifa'i, "Kemal Nefis Sayesinde Bulunur, (Perfection is reached through the *nefis*)," *Ilahiyat-ı Ken'an*, ed. Yusuf Ömürlü and Dinçer Dalkılıç, (Istanbul, 1988), p.68-69.

Q: If Zuleikha can attain perfection, this means that all women have the potential to attain perfection.

A: In one of his poems, 'Attar said, "Zuleikha was sitting by the road through which Joseph was supposed to pass. When she caught sight of Joseph, she let out such a heartfelt cry that the whip (for Joseph's horse) caught fire from her cry. Joseph, unable to carry the whip anymore, threw it away. On seeing this, Zuleikha let out another cry, 'O God! Look at this! He is a great messenger, and I am but a poor woman. Yet when just a little bit of the fire that I carry in my illuminated heart touched his hand, he was unable bear it, and he threw the whip.'" 'Attar continued, "If it weren't for the Zuleikhas of the time, who would know the value of Joseph?" This means if it weren't for the Prophet, how else would God's meaning be known? Annemarie Schimmel, whom I love very much, was an expert on Rumi. In her book titled *My Soul Is a Woman* (which she dedicated to Samiha Ayverdi), she says, "Your spirit is the station of love." In this statement and that of 'Attar's, "woman" represents the *nefis*. When the Prophet said, "I was made to love women," he was referring to the necessity of the *nefis*, without which no spiritual progress is possible. Kenan Rifa'i made the same point when he said, "fragrance means everybody's fragrance, that is, their disposition (*meşreb*; Ar. *mashrab*)."

Q: This is a very important, isn't it? We might understand what women and prayer mean (in the Prophetic statement), but the term "fragrance" conveys an additional detail and it is beautifully expressed.

A: Unless we as a people accept each other's dispositions, there can be no mutual acceptance between us. There is a meaning behind each of the dispositions that God created, which must be understood. Without this understanding, there is no welcoming acceptance amongst people, and they will have a very difficult time reaching *tevhid*. The Prophet says, "In order to do all this, prayer is a must." Only in prayer can these meanings be illuminated; the eye of your illuminated heart starts to see these; prayer is ascension. A companion once told the Prophet that he hated garlic. The Prophet interjected and said, "Don't say you hate garlic; instead, say that you hate its smell. It is forbidden to hate the essence of anything."

Q: When we look at the etymology of "Islam," we see that it comes from the same root as "*taslim* (embrace)," "*muslim* (one who submits)," "*salama* (to accept)"... It means submission to God (having faith in the unseen).

A: There is a very important lesson in sacrificing the pleasures of the *nefis*. Consider the test of Abraham,[7] the decision he took regarding his son, and his son saying, "Father, do as you are commanded." All this tells us that Ishmael, who was at the station of the *nefis*, was ready for these trials. Had he not been ready, there would have been no spiritual ascension. In other words, the *nefis* must be ready. Take, for example, when you go to a psychiatrist. Among the first questions that you are asked are, "Are you ready to cope with your disease? Do you acknowledge that you are ill?" Similarly, is your *nefis* confessing that it is ill? God first and foremost wants this confession from us. Only then does the ascension begin. The words of the *tekbir* – *Allahu Akbar* (God is Great) – protects a person in prayer from worldly thoughts and helps a person declare the desires of the *nefis* as unlawful. And for the people of Truth, the words of the *tekbir* make placing anything beside God unlawful. To say the *tekbir* during prayer is to say, "I have sacrificed myself in Your presence." The submission of Ishmael shows the submission of the *nefis* to the spirit. Only then can the body rid itself of all types of desire. This submission becomes very difficult for people who don't pray. The knowers of God say, "Those who pray are like sacrificial animals cleansed and ready for sacrifice." That is why prayer is indispensable. Now, having said *Bismi'Llah al-rahman al-rahim* (in the Name of God, the most Beneficent, the most Merciful), let us turn to that magnificent chapter of the Qur'an (sura *Fatiha*, The Opening), about which God said, "You can make your prayer with *Fatiha* alone."

Q: Before we turn to sura *Fatiha*, I'd like to ask you a question. We are speaking about *tevhid* from the perspective of Sufism. In doing so, we are also trying to give voice to our illuminated hearts. Earlier, you said that we must accept that different human dispositions have always existed. You said that this is what "fragrance" in the Prophet's saying refers to. So of course while it is clear that on the one hand we ought to respect all dispositions, on the other hand the issue of worship is a very

---

7. In the Muslim tradition it is Ishmael that is said to have been sacrificed by Abraham because he was the first-born son.

contentious topic, particularly with respect to Sufism. Something the famous (late) oncologist Haluk Nurbaki (also a Sufi shaykh) said has stayed with me, and I'd like to ask you about it. Our Prophet said that prayer is the light of his eyes. And if he (the Prophet) is our guide and leader, do we have any right to renounce prayer, while knowing that it was the most beloved of forms of worship for him? Haluk Nurbaki says, "One wonders, was the Prophet less in love with God than those who claim that they are in love with God and renounce prayer? God forbid! He continued with his prayer for his entire life." I wonder what the purpose of love is here.

A: "Our direction (*kıble*; Ar. *qibla*) is the Face of the Beloved, our prayer is continuous / Love is our imam, and the illuminated heart is our community."[8]

In order for a person's prayer to be continuous, as mentioned in the couplet here, and for them to be firm with it, God says, "Even the Prophet is obliged to worship his Beloved with the body." Worship of outward form is the continuation of this state. People of God have performed prayer in various forms. None of the knowers of God, whom I have been humbled to meet and know renounced prayer. On the contrary, the spiritually elevated people of the time increased their prayers. I know that the Prophet used to pray until the morning. My teacher Kenan Rifa'i would perform hundreds of units of prayer each night; he prayed so much that his prayers were as much as they would have been had he been praying since he was one year old. Prayer demonstrates that our connection with the Beloved is not only spiritual; it needs material form. The outer (*zahir*) is the same as the inner (*batin*).

Q: In order to realize the inner meaning of prayer, one has to perform the outer prayer. Is that right?

A: Ibn 'Arabi says, "God manifests through humans, but in order for God's manifestation to occur, humans must first cry out, 'I am a servant, I am a servant!'" This crying out is prayer. A spiritual master like Ibn 'Arabi – who explained the Unity of Existence and the manifestation of God in humans – considers prayer to be of utmost importance. We will discuss the specifics of prayer shortly, including the stages through which we pass and the stations that

8. Yunus Emre, *Divan-i Ilahiyat*, Ed. Mustafa Tatcı, (Istanbul: Kapı Yayınları, 2012).

we reach during prayer. It is known that Mevlana Rumi, the king of love, used to pray until the morning. It has been reported he would prostrate for such long stretches of time that his beard would freeze and stick to the ground of the mosque (Konya is very cold, as you know). They had to use warm water to wash his beard and melt the ice. If these great friends of God never renounced prayer, then who are we to give it up! God Forbid! There is also the verse in the Qur'an in which God says, "I love those who are constant in prayer."[9]

Some exegetes have interpreted this to mean the prayers of the heart. While this is true, God also loves stability and commitment. What He does not love is inconsistency and actions that stem from the *nefis*. If this weren't the case, there might have been a verse in the Qur'an that would state, "Be constant in your prayers until your heart starts praying, and once your heart starts to pray then you can leave your prayers." Is there such a verse in the Qur'an? No. Let me share an anecdote. My mother is an *arif* (possessor of mystical knowledge). Once she met a self-professed Sufi shaykh who held her in high regard and showed her much affection. He said to her, "My daughter, why do you pray? When you pray, there is a separation between you and Him. That is, you worship God as if you were a separate entity from Him. And by doing so, you are practicing dualism." My mother's reply was extraordinary. She said: "You are quite right. But just now, during our conversation, I saw tears rolling down your cheeks. You are in love with God. There is a lover and a Beloved. There is you, and there is God. How can a person fall in love with himself? Why were you crying?" This is the secret. There is unity in duality. There is no unity without duality. Without multiplicity there is no unity.

The first verse of sura *Fatiha* is the *basmala*.[10] The letter "b" in "*Bismi'Llah al-rahman al-rahim*" is the manifestation of God's Names and Attributes in one single body. Which body? The body of the Prophet. "B" means body, and it is a dark, ambiguous letter. If we pass the stage of the letter "b," it is as was said to the Prophet in sura *al-Anfal* (Battle Gains), "When you threw, it wasn't you who threw, but God who threw."[11] If we are purified of our material

---

9. Qur'an, *al-Baqara* (the Cow), (2:238).
10. See "*Fatiha*" in the glossary for a complete translation of this Qur'anic chapter.
11. Qur'an, *al-Anfal* (Battle Gains), (8:17).

existence, we become the dot under the letter "b."[12] Becoming that esteemed dot is the station of 'Ali, who teaches us the meaning of the *basmala*. It is for this station that we give thanks and praise God in sura *Fatiha*. This station teaches us and makes us reflect. God becomes one with His Prophet through His bestowal of compassion and manifestation of mercy. The manifestation of God's mercy is God's enabling us to have the conduct of the Prophet and to be protected by it. This protection feels like living in the next world while still living here.

"*Alhamdu li-'Llahi rabb al-'alamin* (All praise is for God, the Lord of the worlds)." One of the secrets of sura *Fatiha* is hidden in these three words. Declaring that all praise is for the Lord of the worlds starts with praise (*hamd*). That is, it is an implicit, heartfelt plea as if to say, "Teach me praise." There are two very important points in praise. Praise is a greater station than gratitude. It is to be content with whatever may come from God: trouble, trial, sorrow, all of it. It is like saying to God, "O my Beloved! I am happy with everything that comes from You!" But which name of God is addressed here? *Rabb* (Lord).

Q: Yes, God is addressed as the one who teaches and nurtures.

A: Because the word "praise" is from God to God, it is between the meaning of God and the attribute of Lordship, because praise is not a state we can achieve through our individual, carnal souls. For people to receive pain as pleasant and to not have it be painful is only possible with the manifestation of God in them. For example, taking a bitter medicine that will have a healing effect on your illness is a manifestation of Mercy (*al-Rahman*), but not feeling the bitterness and saying, "It is necessary for my healing" is a manifestation of Compassion (*al-Rahim*). The combination of both is praise. Therefore, this teaches us that praise occurs as something from yourself to you, and that this is possible only after prostrating before Adam, namely, the Perfected Human. This prostration means to have the state of Perfected Humans who don't exist with their *nefis* and to adopt qualities like theirs.

Ibn 'Arabi, the Greatest Shaykh, teaches us, "When you are in the standing position during prayer, you earn the rewards of all the trees and walls of the earth, because their state is also that of

---

12. The letter "b" in the Arabic script is transcribed as: "ب"

prayer – this is the connection; when you bend forward, you earn the rewards of all four-legged animals, and when you prostrate, you earn the rewards of all crawling animals, plants and herbs. The meaning of their worship manifests in you, and you acquire all their rewards. Mind you, we gain all this during prayer." This is the attribute of Mercy. Everything worships, and everything is attracted to God. To comprehend the meaning of God, that is called witnessing.

Q: It is the attraction of a single dot, is it not?

A: In science, we call this affinity, or the power of attraction. In the entire macro and micro cosmos, there is the manifestation of mercy, love, and attraction. The affinity between iron and oxygen is an example of the manifestation of Mercy. The world – which constitutes movement – emerges from this attraction. Compassion manifests. Why? With Mercy there is love. God's protection for His creation is as capacious as the love that permeates the mother's womb. Compassion keeps the world and the entire universe under His protection. Those who praise and thank their Lord sense His protection. His Compassion is for those who give praise; it is a sublime attribute; it is comparable to our mother's bosom; it is, so to speak, the mother's bosom opened to us by God. Compassion is the bosom of love. In the phrase, "He is the most Beneficent, the most Merciful," God reminds us of these two truths that belong to Him and that have become manifest in His Prophet. The *Fatiha* is a chapter of the Qur'an that is recited half by God and half by the servant. It is a chapter that is shared by God and the servant.

Q: This is quite extraordinary.

A: Yes. Next is "the Master of the Day of Judgment." God is the Master of the Day of Judgment. What does that mean? It refers to the moment you rise to your feet and stand in the presence of God. The meaning of God becomes manifest in you in this standing position (*kiyam*; Ar. *qiyam*). God warns us not to attribute this to ourselves; He is its Master. This is a very important point. We will be called to account for our deeds. He will ask, "I gave you hands and feet. What did you sow? Did you cultivate your body? Did you find meaning? Did you uncover your treasure? I am the Master of that day." What day is that day? It is the day when human beings will say, "I am nothing and He is everything." God says, "That happens with My blessing alone." Here He reminds us of His meaning. We now move to a very important point.

Q: The servant starts to speak?

A: Yes. If we pay close attention, we will see that *Şeriat*, *Tarikat* (Sufi path), and *Hakikat* (Truth) are hidden in these verses of the *Fatiha*. To be at the level of *Şeriat* is to say, "You alone do we worship," which is to say, "There is me and there is You. I worship You with my *nefis*, thinking it's from me and attributing the power of worship to myself while asking for your help." To be on the *Tariqa* or the path of Sufism is to say, "When left alone, I am nothing. I perform my servitude only with Your help." The mere thought of this (nothingness) arrests perfected humans at the core of their being. Addressing His servants, God says, "O tongue! You say you are in My presence and seek my help, and claim to worship Me. But the limbs that appointed you as their representative commit slander; they are heedless of Me. You are lying when you say, 'You alone do I worship and from You alone do we seek help.'" Possessors of mystical knowledge tremble at the thought that their words will be thrown back at them with the rebuke, "You're lying!" So they are very relieved if and when they manage to move on to the next verse: *ihdina al-sirat al-mustaqim* (guide us to the Straight Path).

According to Ibn 'Arabi, the tongue is the translator and spokesperson for the eyes, the ears, the hands, the feet, the abdomen, the heart, and all the rest of the body during prayer. It is for this reason that possessors of mystical knowledge regard this part of the prayer as the most dangerous. They say that at this stage of prayer, if a person is in the presence (of God) with his entire existence, and if that person directs himself to God with his entire being, just as the tongue says (You alone do I worship, and from You alone do we seek help), then prayer becomes spiritual ascent (*mirac*) for him. As for the straight path, the one who is already on the straight path takes over, and the task is made easier, and this is what *mirac* means: "Make my feet firm on Your Path." This is the Truth. This path is not just any path. This is a straight and continuous path. In this world, for someone to be steadfast on the Straight Path, they have to embody the ethical conduct (*ahlak*) of their spiritual teacher and the Prophet. This is the straight path. Moreover, the people of knowledge consider being stable on the path "the greatest miracle." To be firm-footed, not give up, and not say, "I haven't been able to perfect my manner and make progress on the path. I quit, I can no longer follow the path." To not throw away the sword of action – that is the Straight Path and its end, which is *tevhid*. That is why the Prophet's Straight Path is *tevhid*. May God allow us to achieve this.

The rest of the *Fatiha* is a heartfelt plea, "Lead us to the path of those whom You have favored and not of those who have incurred Your wrath nor of those who are astray." The word "astray" in the original represents the station of Christianity, which refers to someone who is stuck in love and unable to reach unity, or to the idolizing of form and forsaking of knowledge. It also represents the station of Judaism, at which one dwells in knowledge, or gets stuck at knowledge without love; the term *"maghdubi 'alayhim"* (those who have incurred Your wrath) represents the people of this station.

The verses recited after the *Fatiha* turn the inner meaning of the *Fatiha* into embodied experience. The worshipper moves into the bowing position. This gesture signals the shame one feels in responding to God's question, "I created you naked and gave you intellect and understanding; what have you brought to Me?" Rumi phrased this question of God in the following way: "Where and why did you shed your tears? How did you spend your life? I granted you hands and feet so that you could sow from the soil of your body. What have you produced?" In response to this divine address, we pronounce three times, *"Subh"ana Rabbiyu'l-'azim* (Praise be to the Mightiest Lord)." With the first pronunciation, we declare God to be above all human conceptions of God (*tenzih*); in the second pronunciation, we declare God to be above all the attributes with which He is associated (*teshbih*). With the third pronunciation, we affirm incomparability (*tenzih*) and similitude (*teshbih*). We declare both of these truths about Him. We say, "You are above all our ideas about You." Does this mean we no longer imagine who God is? Of course we do; in fact "prayer" is our understanding of God, an understanding that corresponds to our own eyes and spiritual capacities. But it is proper to refrain from depicting Him with a specific image. We should think of Him as infinite and eternal. This is just such a moment, that is, a moment of displaying etiquette (*edep*), because we are in the position of bowing (*rüku*).

The servant repeats this beautiful declaration while in the bowing position, and after affirming God's greatness and his own nothingness, God calls out to him, "Hold your head up and offer praise." Here, only those who have attained the truth of their prayer can say, "*Rabbana laka'l-hamd* (All praise is for You alone)." First he stands up, but having no strength left, he falls in prostration and asks to be granted God's mercy. While in prostration he says "*Subhana Rabbiyu'l-a'la* (Praise be to the elevated Lord)" three times. The first utterance means, "I declare my Lord to be above all the beauty of attributes." The meaning of *Tenzih,* or the state of affirming God's incomparability, takes on an altogether different dimension here. The second utterance means, "I declare my God to be above all the beauty that I am able to comprehend." The third utterance is to say, "I declare my God to be above all beauty that I might perceive." Whilst in prostration, the servant perceives his non-existence; God asks him, "O my servant, I have given you abundant blessings, where are the fruits of these blessings?" After the second prostration, he sit on his knees, and listens to this question. If he has reached his ascension during the prostrations (that is, if he has understood his nothingness), then he recites salutations to God (*ettahiyyatu*; Ar. *al-tahiyya*) with meaning. This is the moment about which the Prophet said, "There was nothing else between God and me."

What does the deliverance of salutations mean? It means to remember, mention, and extend thanks for the Prophet who allows us to understand all this, and for the experiences we are able to have through worship. There are three very important sentences in the salutations. The first sentence is either said by the spirit or to the spirit, which is God's breath and command. The second sentence is addressed to the Prophet, which is the illuminated heart. The third sentence is said by our soul. This is the sentence that draws us back to the world. Prayer ends with the chapters in the Qur'an that the Prophet recited from time to time. Now we return to the world, and if we performed our prayer with beauty then we feel happy. In the *Mathnawi,* Mevlana says prayer is "Judgment day;" if the servants are unable to answer the questions put to them, they turn their heads to the right, seeking help from friends of God and from the prophets. If the servant is still in this world, the friends of God tell the servant, 'I can help you; I have accepted you; I have taken you to the Hereafter from your *mirac.* But in the next world, nothing and no one can help you except God.' The servant then turns his head to the left and seeks help from the things he worshipped in the world. Those things that he worshipped then say to him – if he is still in this world – 'We thank you for your loyalty to us, but as you know none of us can help you.' In the afterlife, they tell him, 'We cannot help you in any way. What good did you derive in the world from worshipping us?'"

The servant is now left alone with his God; he holds up his hands, opens his palms, and supplicates. We know that prostration is a way to subdue the *nefis* that establishes itself as a ruler over us. Prostration destroys the *nefis*. The *nefis* considers itself a sovereign; in the same way that a sovereign views all people in a society as his servants, so does the *nefis*, as though it were a god. Prostration also marks the servant's realization of his own nothingness, and his finding the perfect guide who is the manifestation of the Real King.

I want to mention two types of prostrations here, and I will explain them further below. Let us return to the topic of Adam. Since Adam was honored with divine blessings, he possessed the essence of love. But in eating the forbidden apple of love, he erred. He felt great pain because of this mistake. Eventually, however, he became a dutiful servant. He recognized his nothingness and reached the station of prophethood. He attributed his error to himself, regarding it as a particular rather than an essential mistake and said to God, "The mistake was mine, your servant's." This admission earned him the rank of prophethood. God commanded Satan to prostrate before Adam. But Satan fell to drawing comparisons between him and Adam, and defiantly declared, "I was created of fire, and he of clay. Fire is superior to clay. So why should I prostrate to him?" This arrogance made Satan from among the rejected ones. Moreover, he tried to blame God and said, "I possess no power or will; it is You who does and makes us do anything. If You had so willed, You would have made me prostrate!"

Intellect alone is not enough to comprehend God's meaning and commands. Intellectual understanding must be accompanied with right conduct (*edep*). *Edep* means the ability to see God's meaning in all of God's creation. If *Şeriat* and Sufism don't go together, true meaning will not become manifest. Prayer represents the moment when a servant understands his limits. Like Satan, we too might be inclined to say, "Why do I need prayer? If You had so willed, You would have made me do it." "I love you very much; why do we need to get married? Let's continue our relationship as it is." Prayer is like a spiritual wedding. We understand our limits during prayer and say, "we are servants." This is one of the most beautiful meanings of prayer. God commanded all the angels to prostrate before Adam, the master of the moment. That was the first prostration to be performed after God commanded prostration. All the angels prostrated before Adam without the slightest hesitation. This is the meaning of the first prostration. They then looked up, saw the light on Adam's face, and prostrated again. This was the second prostration, the prostration of the mystical state (*hal*). The first prostration was that of Şeriat, the second of Divine Reality. Some of the spirits however, did not respond to the command of the first prostration. Even so, they saw the light on Adam's face and made the second prostration. They first denied God's Şeriat and resisted submitting. A second group made the first prostration but stopped there, and in doing so settled for Şeriat. Thus they fulfilled the command externally but didn't understand its meaning. Hence they did not perform the second prostration since they could not see the light on Adam's face. This manner of praying does not lead a person to the station of witnessing. A third group made both prostrations. They are the knowers, friends, and prophets of God. How fortunate they are. May God allow us to be with them at all times. Prostration during prayer reminds us of the joyous moment in pre-eternity when we cried, "Yes, we bear witness!" to the question "Am I not your Lord?" Prayer brings together unity of God, reminder of God's existence, prostration to God, and the secret of the proclamation, "We bear witness" from pre-eternity.

Q: We experience the state we were once in when we said, "Yes, we bear witness" in pre-eternity. When you spoke about the importance of prostration earlier, you said that we are not alone when we pray, that the trees and even the walls around us pray with us. Isn't prostration the most critical element of every society? Historically, Muslims have always prostrated before God; but then even pagans have made similar gestures before their idols. For this reason, the first rule of prostration is to say "I have submitted," in other words, to be Ishmael for our prayer and for our life. Of course you know this better, that prostration is not limited to human beings. God says in sura *al-Nahl* (the Bee), "Do the [disbelievers] not observe the things that God has created, casting their shadows right and left, submitting themselves to God obediently?"[13] In addition to the angels, all living things in the heavens and the earth also prostrate themselves before God. They are not arrogant about any good deed that they do. To go back to the meaning of prostration, just as we work on our *nefis* and sacrifice our desires during prayer, do we not destroy arrogance – one of the seven deadly sins – during prostration?

A: I heard a talk by an artist the other day. He said, "I pray in order to express my nothingness before God and to be able to prostrate." I liked his answer very much. What a wonderful thought. This is prostration. When I was studying what it means to prostrate the self, I remember coming across the saying of a gnostic who said, "those who deliberately renounce prayer unknowingly reduce themselves in the eyes of God to a level lower than that of those who prostrate before an idol, even though they are not Muslims."

Q: Our day begins and ends with prayer. It strikes me as particularly interesting that our religious festivities also begin with prayer; for instance, *Eid al-Fitr* and *Eid al-Adha*. The meaning of these days has a deeper significance with prayer, which is itself a celebration for those who reflect. Can we discuss this further? Why do we pray during religious festivities?

A: Prayers performed on such special days are about love and gratitude. It is to say, "I have fulfilled the duty that was due on me from Your blessing, and I now declare my love for You with this prayer." During spiritual sermons such as at the time of Eid prayers and other religious gatherings, the fire of love passes from person to person. Let me relate a *hadith* of the Prophet to illustrate this point. The Prophet said: "Shake hands without gloves." I have learnt that love and knowledge are transmitted from the veins of the palm of one's hand to the heart. So when you shake hands with someone from among the people of love, if you are sincere and have the right intention, then it is God's love that is transmitted to you from that single handshake. Let me recount another *hadith* of the Prophet: "Make your rows during congregational prayer as close together as possible." This means that the pleasure of worship and the meaning inherent in worship travels from one worshipper to another. It can also mean that we taste spiritual pleasure together

13. Qur'an, *al-Nahl* (the Bee), (16:48). Tr. Haleem, *Qur'an*, p. 169.

by praying slowly and behind an Imam. For this reason, it is very important that we welcome religious festivities and all other spiritually uplifting events with prayer.

Before we conclude our talk on prayer, I'd like to add that the Perfected Human says, "The Prophet made a request that divine peace and blessings be upon his people (the same request we recite in our salutations). As a result of this request of the Prophet, if the prayer of a servant is performed with its inner meaning, then he is taken to the stations of the content self (*raziye*; Ar. *radiyya*) and the self-pleasing to God (*merdiye*; Ar. *mardiyya*)." What are these two stations? *Radiyya* is when we are content with God and grateful for all that He gives. In return, if God wills, He will make us pleasing to Himself. Then God speaks to us, as in the Qur'anic verse, "Return to your Lord well-pleased, and well-pleasing to Him."[14] The servant continues to struggle – remember that work is also prayer. Understanding this point is essential. The servant reaches the highest station, well-pleased and well-pleasing to Him. If, with God's blessing, he reaches the station of Unity of Actions (*fi'il tevhidi*), all his deeds and words belong to God and he sees all of creation through the attributes of the Truth. He continues his efforts unceasingly, reaches the station of Attributes, and if he perseveres on this path, the Essence is unveiled to Him. Here, he hears the divine address, "O My Servant! I am pleased with you, are you pleased with Me too?" On hearing this, he perseveres even more. This is the meaning of prayer.

Q: I recently picked up Osman Kemali Effendi's collection of poems.[15] On opening the book, I opened to page one hundred and twenty four, where the following couplet spoke to me:

"O ascetic! If you seek God, the heart is His evidence
It is the abode of the All-Merciful; seek and find God therein."

A: 'Ali said, "I don't worship a God whom I cannot see." The ability to see God is realized during prayer. Mevlana Rumi said, "Prayer is a light in one's heart. Those who wish can illuminate themselves with it. The key that opens the door of paradise is prayer. It is the pillar of religion; whoever renounces it renounces their

---

14. Sura *al-Fajr* (Daybreak), (89:28).
15. Osman Kemali Efendi, *Kemali Divanı'ndan Aşk Sızıntıları*, Ed. Baha Doğramacı, (Istanbul: Divan Matbaacılık, 1977).

religion and faith as well. Whoever establishes it establishes their religion and goes to the next world as a believer." In sura *al-Mu'minun* (Believers) it mentions,"those who pray humbly," (being overwhelmed by the awe and majesty of God) and "those who are ever mindful guardians of their Prayers."[16] And as you know, the Prophet gave the good news, "I will intercede for those who pray." There can be no greater news than this.

When asked to comment on prayer, the Prophet said, "If there was a river flowing outside your door, and you bathed in it five times a day, would any dirt be left on your body?" His companions answered, "No, there would be no dirt left, O Messenger of God." "So, the five prayers are similar to this. God forgives your sins with prayer." The time of each prayer is also very important, as people are being invited to God. The morning prayer is when people are given physical and spiritual abilities. A person must be awake at that time to be able to give thanks, as if to say, "I am able to wake up, I have been given the faith and power to worship You. You have given me physical ability as well as granted me with spiritual ability." A person gets up and is united with His Beloved. This is a very joyful moment.

The morning prayer, which is probably the most important of all prayers, is also a way to express gratitude for the manifestation of the Prophet, which took place during a time of immense tribulation. It is also to give thanks for the moment when one is taken out from darkness and heedlessness to (a life of) meaning. Do you see what kinds of things we are reminded of by the morning prayer? It is as if at that time, the angel Michael (Mika'il) distributes our entire spiritual blessing to us. Speaking about the outer benefits of prayer, Bernard Shaw, the famous British author, considered prayer as a prescription for the twenty-first century. It is the sustenance that prepares a person for the rest of the day. The blessing and nourishment of each day comes from the morning prayer.

The noon prayer is a reminder that jolts us when we are preoccupied with our work. It says, "Stop, O traveler! Where are you going? Will all this work that you immerse yourself in take you anywhere? To work as a service to humanity is fine, but how sad if the only aim is to benefit yourself!"

The Qur'an says the afternoon prayer is the middle prayer

---

16. Qur'an, *al-Mu'minun* (Believers), (23:2) and (23:9).

and is very important; afternoon is when people are distracted. If you're tired you will be given strength; at that moment, there is a God Who reminds you of Himself.

Then comes the evening (dusk) prayer. It will get dark and the hardships will begin. A short evening prayer prepares us for these challenges and prevents us from being forgetful.

Finally with the night prayer we complete the day with a supplication like, "Even as I am preparing to go to bed, keep me with You. Acquaint my spirit with the meaning of the pre-eternal realm." The five daily prayers keep this regime going. But what should we be most attentive to while praying? Let me quote one of Mevlana Rumi's heartfelt pleas to God; it is from the second volume of the *Mathnawi*:

> My God! If I don't offer my heart to you completely, then I don't consider this prayer to be prayer. It is because of your love that I turned my face to the direction of prayer. Without you, what would I do with prayer and the *kible,* which otherwise only make me weary? O God, I feel ashamed at my prayer that is full of hypocrisy. Shame prevents me from entering my heart; I cannot find you. Truthfully, the one who performs his prayer in its true meaning must have the attributes of an angel, but I am still a monster. If a person's clothes touch a dog, they cannot pray unless the clothes are cleaned. But here I carry the dog of my soul in my arms. Please accept my prayer. Through prayer I strive to find you in my heart and to be with you, so that I can then stop speaking of the pain of separation. How can I call this prayer when while my face is turned towards the prayer niche (*mihrab*), my heart is in the bazar?

This is the kind of prayer that the people of knowledge recommend to us. A man once entered a mosque. He saw the sultan praying inside and said, "greetings to my sultan!" This angered the sultan very much, and on completing his prayer, he shouted, "Don't you know that you cannot greet someone in the middle of their prayer! You forgetful one!" The man, who was a gnostic, replied, "If you had actually been in the middle of prayer, I would not have greeted you. But while praying, you were wondering what color you should paint the walls of your palace. My aim was to bring you back to your prayer by greeting you." Prayer is where humans most frequently run into Satan. It is the time for a person to be alone with him or herself; it is when a person is most aware of his status as a servant, of his nothingness, of his shortcomings. One day, Satan was waiting outside the mosque. A person who was about to enter the mosque recognized him and asked, "O Satan, what are you doing here?" "I'm planning to deceive that man who is praying. But the problem is that I can't enter the mosque!" "Why?" the man asked, and Satan replied, "There is a gnostic taking a nap over there and I am very afraid of him!" If we are able to pray in the same way as that sleeping gnostic, then prayer enables us to reach his state. For many years, Hanafi performed the morning prayer with the same ablution that he had done for his night prayer. Even in his sleep he enjoyed the unity and togetherness with God.

Ibn ʿArabi says, "Performing prayer in its outer form earns a person a spiritual station in this world. But performing prayer with meaning brings nearness and allows the person to reach the degree of Mustafa." It is the blessing of this intimacy that matters the most. I am often asked about its meaning, and I usually explain it through my experience as a teacher. A teacher, out of pity, passes a student who regularly does his homework but doesn't fully understand the material. The point is that even if we can't perform prayer in an ideal state and do not comprehend the meaning of prayer at each moment, we should still perform it in its outer form so that on the Day of Judgment we can find the strength to say to God, "Even as I was not able to attain its meaning, I did my homework. As a teacher, I took pity on the students who didn't complete their assignments and passed them. O Lord, please do the same with me." Prayer is a form of worship, the meaning of which multiplies when we talk about it. This is what we have been discussing. May God forgive me for my shortcomings and may He make my prayer a spiritual state for me and make the prayers of all Muslims a spiritual state for them. I'd like to add one last thing: Istanbul is a sublime city that unites two directions of prayer. That is, when you face the Kaʿba from Istanbul, you also face Masjid al-Aqsa. It is only Istanbul's unique privilege that it unites these two at the same time. May God allow us to understand this.

Q: While praying, we turn towards the Kaʿba. Wherever we may be in the world, we have only one direction. Can you say more about this as we conclude?

A: Turning one's face towards the Ka'ba is one of the conditions of prayer. But this gesture also has inner meanings. While some may find this reading puzzling, in truth, we are prostrating to each other's illuminated hearts. Turning towards the Ka'ba ensures praying in congregation; that is what makes it important. With regards to its inner meaning, it is said in sura *al-Baqara* (The Cow), "Take care to do your prayers, praying in the best way, and stand before God in devotion."[17] The continuous prayer is the prayer of the illuminated heart, and its direction is the heart of the Prophet – that is, the one who has taught us its meaning. What this means is this: just as you turn towards the Ka'ba when you pray, you also prostrate yourself before the Prophet or the spiritual teacher who taught you the teachings of the Prophet. Prostration here signifies paying one's debt of loyalty. Prostrate before the spiritual teacher who reflects the meaning of God in the present so you may remember God's command to Adam to prostrate. Please don't misunderstand what I just said; it is not that we prostrate ourselves before human beings, but rather before the meaning of humans such as the Prophet and spiritual teacher. Prostrating before a human being is idolatry, God forbid! What we prostrate to is the meaning, the meaning of that lion which becomes manifest in the tiniest of bodies; it is to that meaning that we prostrate. If you're prostrating to that meaning, then do it. But if not, and you see the object of prostration as a human being, then don't prostrate, or else you will be led to disbelief. The goal of prostrating to Adam is not to bow before him. Rather it is to cultivate faith in what he says, to do as he tells us to do, and to avoid what he tells us to avoid.

---

17. Qur'an, *al-Baqara* (the Cow), (2:238). Tr. Haleem, *Qur'an*, p. 27.

Chapter Six:
Pilgrimage and Sacrifice (Hajj ve Kurban)

Q: What is the meaning of the sacrifice of animals during the *Hajj*?

A: Before we move to the subject of sacrifice, I want to read what our teacher said in relation to the *Hajj*. He quoted a couplet from the *Mathnawi*:

> Ever since God's abode has existed, God has not lived in it.
> In my heart, however, there is nothing but the Ever-living One.

> The Ka'ba is a building of the Friend, the son of Azar
> The heart is the building of the Greatest Majestic One

The Ka'ba is the building of *Khalil* (Abraham), the Friend, the son of Azar. The heart, however, is the secluded cell of God. Everything that exists in the material realm exists in the spiritual realm too. All material existence manifests in order to point to the spiritual meaning. And all of existence also exists in the human being. For example, what are Moses and Pharaoh? Do they not represent the struggle between the spirit and the soul? Moses and Pharaoh continue their battle. And this conflict will continue until Judgment Day.

Qur'anic verses and other signs exist in order for us to know what lies within the human being. Kenan Rifa'i says, "Each verse of the Qur'an is a story written for the purpose of communicating to us our inner meaning and our problems. We must never mistake Qur'anic stories for children's stories, nor to make the mistake of regarding the *Mathnawi* as a compilation of love stories and fables.

Each narrative is an outward reflection of events that we experience within ourselves. Numerous signs of God exist and manifest in the universe. These are all collected and collated in the human being. In sura *al-Dhariyat* (Scattering [Winds]) God says, "Everything is within you (in your *nefis*). Don't you see any of these?"

The face of the beloved is the beauty and magnificence of God.

Those who perform the *Hajj* circumambulate the Ka'ba that is constructed from stones and soil. When a person circumambulates the Ka'ba, he is in fact circling around the true meaning of the Beloved rather than around stones. To go to the Ka'ba, people wear the *ihram*, the pure white garments. In other words, they take off their clothes. The lovers who pursue the Ka'ba with an illuminated heart are stripped of both worlds. Thus, what this act requires is that the person strips themselves of both worlds.

Pleasing an illuminated heart is the greatest *Hajj*. One illuminated heart is better than a thousand Ka'bas.

In other words, this requires leaving the burdens, hypocrisies, and temptations of the world behind and not agonizing over questions like, "Am I going to Heaven?" or "Am I living with the fear of Hell?" or "Am I a good or a bad person?" The Ka'ba is the place of God's contentment because a person goes there to attain God's contentment. The heart, on the other hand, is where God is witnessed and beheld. It is where God is seen. Therefore, an illuminated heart is greater than the heavens and the earth, the world and the universe, and the sacred Ka'ba itself. How happy is the person who finds a gnostic, who is the true Mount Arafat bearing witness to God's beauty. Such an enlightened person does not witness anything but the meaning of God.

Is there only one road that leads to the Ka'ba?

Of course not. There are roads that lead to the Ka'ba from all over the world. Pilgrims' paths vary from Africa, America, and Asia, while the meeting place and goal is one, and that is the Ka'ba. Just as these roads vary in difficulty, length, and comfort depending on the location of the pilgrim, so too do the roads leading to God. The journey to God will vary from long to short, difficult to easy, according to the traveler's ability granted to him or her from before eternity.

A *hadith* states, "The remembrance of 'Ali is worship." Why is it worship to remember 'Ali? 'Ali was completely consumed in the Truth. To cast your gaze on the Ka'ba means to look upon the beautiful face of 'Ali, and the faces of Perfected Humans. Remembering all Perfected Humans who have embodied the secret of 'Ali is considered worship. This *hadith* is not only devoted to 'Ali. Any Perfected Human who carries the meaning of 'Ali is at the same station as 'Ali. To remember a beloved of God is pleasing to God.

A story from the *Mathnawi* recounts that a king had many servants. One of those servants loved the king dearly. When this servant would go to see the king, everyone would put letters into his pockets without him realizing. He would go before the king with his pockets filled with wishes for the beloved. However, the moment the servant would see his beloved- the king- he would faint. The king liked this very much and said, "Let me see what this servant who loves me so much has brought in his pockets. Let me read and grant these wishes." Mevlana says: "O heedless one! If you are going to ask something from God, put your letter in the pocket of such a servant that is in love with Him." That is to say, find a Perfected Human and stay close to him. The Perfected Human will advance on the path by being in the presence of His beloved. He will go to God in such a state that God will grant your wishes for his sake.

> Q: In *Fihi Ma-Fihi*, Rumi says, "God fulfills all the duties of His lovers because He desires them. Just as the lover says, 'If God wills, I will enter,' God responds, 'If the Beloved wills.'"[1]

A: Perfected Humans have been honored with God's manifestation. The lines on their faces are like the calligraphy of the Qur'an, which Kenan Rifa'i refers to as the "*kalimatu'Llah* (words of God)." The Qur'an states, "Say [Prophet], 'If the whole ocean were ink for

---

1. The reference is to a passage from Rumi's *Fihi ma fihi*, which describes the lovers of God as exceptional "inasmuch as a lover does not see himself as in control or as an agent with free will; a lover considers himself as subject to the beloved's control. Therefore, he says, 'If the beloved wishes, let us enter.' Now the holy temple, in the view of the externalists, is that Kaaba to which people go; but for lovers and the elite it is union with God. Therefore, they say, 'If God please, let us reach Him and be honored by seeing Him.' On the other hand, it is rare for the beloved to say, 'If God please.' It is like a stranger's tale, which requires a stranger to listen or to be able to listen. God has servants who are beloved and loved and who are sought by God, who performs all the duties of a lover with respect to them. Just as a lover would say, 'If God please, we will arrive,' God says, 'If God please' on behalf of that stranger." See *Signs of the Unseen: the Discourses of Jalal al-Din Rumi*, Tr. Wheeler Thackston, (Putney, VT: Threshold Books, 1994), p. 104.

writing the words of my Lord, it would run dry before those words were exhausted' – even if We were to add another ocean to it."[2] The light of truth shines on the face of Perfected Humans.

The Ka'ba was by the command of God built from stones and soil. Only His command resides in the Ka'ba, whereas God Himself thrives in the heart of the Perfected Human. In a *hadith qudsi*, God says: "I cannot be contained in the whole cosmos, yet the heart of a true believer can contain Me." Consequently, to observe God's Perfected Humans is a form of worship. The purpose of worship is to love God with commitment and devotion. To love those whom God loves is to love God Himself.

Either the heart needs to reach God or we need to give our heart to someone who has already reached God. Love and faith are not acquired by reciting *"hu"* in vain. Loving the Household of the Prophet and following their path means to gain their good pleasure. Love for them is possible only by following their path. If you claim to have jumped as far as forty yards in Baghdad, people will demand proof for you to substantiate your statement. When Ahmed Rifa'i's son said he loved him, Ahmed Rifa'i exclaimed, "If you don't follow my path and the path of the beloved of God, I will deny that you are my son on the Day of Judgment." However, if such a son follows his father's path, he will be light upon light (*nur 'ala nur*).

The Prophet said about Salman Farsi: "Salman is my family." My teacher says, "It doesn't matter if you are a descendant of the Prophet (*sayyid* or *sherif*). Unless you follow their path and earn that honor, of what use is it?" As stated in the verses of the Qur'an, you will not be judged in the afterlife on the basis of your wealth, possessions or children. Lineage is of no value there. The Prophet said, "The best and most honorable among you in the sight of God are the ones who are the most pious."

There is nothing in this world that is not honored by the light of God. Niyazi-i Mısri says that at the Ka'ba, in the house of idols, at home, and in desolate places do I cry, "O friend, O friend."

"La mawjuda illa'Llah (except God nothing exists)." For those who know and can see, every place is the Ka'ba. A priest had once come to see Mevlana, and Mevlana escorted him to the door. The people around him asked why he did that, implying that a priest

---

2. Qur'an, *al-Kahf* (the Cave), (18:109). Tr. Haleem, Qur'an, p. 190.

was not worthy of Mevlana's attention. Mevlana replied, "I am not honoring his priesthood, but the light of God that I see in him." My late teacher used to say that no matter where that light is, it can be sensed and seen. Thus, let us pray that God enables us to circumambulate the Ka'ba with this meaning and intent.

> Q: Moving to the subject of sacrifice; if sacrifice means a thing that helps us get closer to God, do we need to understand sura *Kawthar* (Abundance) in order to understand its real meaning?

A: *Kawthar* is one of the most powerful chapters of the Qur'an, as it gives glad tidings. God says, "I have sent this chapter to the mothers of those who have lost their children." I myself, as a mother who lost her child, try to embody its meaning, and the glad tidings that it gives lift my spirit and please my heart. Let me start by discussing the context in which this chapter was revealed.

When the Prophet lost his last son Abraham, the polytheists around him were very happy; they said, "Your offspring is now cut off, O Muhammad!" In other words, you have no successors left. The Prophet was deeply saddened by this and his heart was distressed. The lineage mentioned here is not a reference to his physical lineage rather spiritual. After this, God reassured him that his lineage would continue through the line of Fatima. "O Muhammad, your offspring is not cut off, it will continue." In other words, this chapter means that the lineage of the Prophet will continue through his daughter Fatima, and that any claim that tries to refute this will be cut and will eventually disappear.

Let us parse out the meaning word by word: "We have granted you *Kawthar*." That is, We have granted you the meaning of God. We have sent His infinite meaning through the Prophet. That meaning is eternal. "So, pray to your Lord and sacrifice." If you understand even a part of this, and you know the source of your existence, you will realize your non-existence. So pray, confirm your status as God's servant, bow your head, prostrate, and sacrifice. That is, sacrifice the excessive desires of your *nefis*. "For he who hates you, he will be cut off." That is, the eternal meaning (that gives you life) is never cut off. God says, "you are the conveyor of the meaning of My eternity, O Muhammad." He further says, "those who don't know you and are heedless of you will perish, and this is a well-deserved end for them."

Q: What is the real meaning of the water of *Kawthar*?

A: Mevlana uses *Kawthar* to symbolize the Perfected Human. The Perfected Human restores the organs of people that burn in the hell-fire of lust.

Who is the Perfected Human who is the master of *Kawthar*? Mevlana uses the term drowning (*istigrak*) when he speaks about the Perfected Human. For Mevlana, drowning represents the state of a bee when it is immersed in the honey that it has produced. That person is at the station of the bee – lost in the fountain of honey or *Kawthar*, which carries the meaning of the Perfected Human. Like the bee, he is immersed in the honey. He is immersed in the meaning of God and the light of Muhammad, which is his own meaning. While his character remains unchanged (he is still a bee), his movements are determined by the honey in which it is immersed. For example, if there is a ripple in the honey, then the bee is able to move its wings. So we can say that every movement that comes from the Perfected Human is a manifestation of God's meaning.

Q: Does the verse, "The hand that threw wasn't yours, it was My hand" carry the same meaning?

A: Yes, this is exactly that state. In other words, it is the Perfected Human who is the manifestation of the essence of God. So the admiration that we have for the Perfected Human is not for that person, but for the Essence. My teacher was discussing this with one of his students, and he explained it in the following way: His student said to him, "I love you very much, my teacher." This was a young girl. The teacher asked, "My daughter, what do you love about me? My eyebrows? Eyes? Mustache? Or my beard?" The student said no to all of the above. "If you loved these," he said, "You would have been mistaken, because these things will eventually disappear. If you like the way I speak, you would again be wrong, because if an illness strikes me, my speech might disappear. If you like the coherence of my words, teachings, and actions, and the manner in which they never contradict the Qur'an, that too doesn't belong to me. It belongs to God. That is why all of this means you love God." A Perfected Human is the one who displays God in him at all times. He is the bridge that takes a person to God. In chemistry, this is the role played by the catalyst. The catalyst is matter that doesn't enter into a reaction; it merely accelerates a chemical reaction. A spiritual guide only accelerates or helps a person to advance, and purifies them of their ugly traits. The guide does not enter the process; he subsumes the person in his own meaning.

Q: Water has a purifying property. With ablution we cleanse our physical body. Does our inner self get purified by the words of a Perfected Human?

A: Yes, that is very true. The process of cleansing our physical body with ablution also carries a deeper meaning. When we spoke about prayer, pilgrimage, and worship, we began with the meaning of ablution. Let us consider ablution in the context of sacrifice. Ablution means to cleanse oneself of the imperfections of the realm of the universe. It means removing imperfections through divine manifestation, because water is the secret of life. Water is our meaning. Everything was created from water, as the *Qur'an* says. Therefore, we cleanse our inner selves from flaws and imperfections that have been acquired over time with the very source of creation. A person appears to clean his or her body with ablution, but the real cleansing and protection from sin comes with prayer and good deeds. So water has two meanings: water that cleanses (a) the body and (b) our inner selves.

Let us divide the water that cleans our inner self into: (i) worship and good deeds; and (ii) love and tears.

These two are considered the instruments for cleansing the inner self. Water is required to cleanse oneself of the flaws, failings, defects, and deficiencies of the heart and *nefis*; their bad *ahlak* (conduct) has to adopt the divine *ahlak* (conduct).

Mevlana Rumi starts his *Mathnawi* with the word "Listen" because the word that enters the ear is the road that leads to the heart. So it cleanses, purifies, and gratifies the person. Without cleansing oneself with tears from the spring of love and affection, and unifying the four *tekbirs*, the meaning of worship would not manifest.

Q: What does unifying the four *tekbirs* mean?

A: To unify the four *tekbirs* means to abandon this world, to abandon the hereafter, to abandon existence, and to abandon abandonment. Abandoning the world does not mean to isolate the self and not have any cares about, say, material and physical comforts. Abu al-Hasan al-Shadhili, who was a Perfected Human, has said: "Wear nice clothes, look good. That is how you will show your gratitude for the blessings that God gave you." So beautification is a form of worship. Abandoning the world does not mean to isolate the self, rather to do away with feeling sad for this world and free oneself from worrying thoughts such as, "What will become of me? Why did I make this mistake yesterday? What will become of my children?" The meaning of "to abandon" in this context is on the one hand to submit to God's wishes, and on the other hand, to keep up one's own striving.

To abandon the hereafter is to cease avoiding sins for the sake of entering heaven, because God says, "Refrain from what I have forbidden to you because of your love for me." In other words, don't refrain for the sake of reward. This is a very high station.

To abandon existence is to abandon your boastful existence. This is the hardest part: to stop saying "I" all the time, an oft repeated exercise when we explain our actions and supposed accomplishments. But the real question is, "What do we really achieve on our own?" We are mere faucets. If God does not turn the faucet, what words can ever flow from us? The greatest scholars can lose their knowledge to the scourge of Alzheimer's. What good are our faculties and abilities? What power do we really have? If a stomachache or an ailment afflicts us, we cannot speak or even worship. That is why abandoning existence is a high station.

After you abandon all of these, there is nothing left to abandon. Everywhere becomes God. Then a person abandons abandonment. That is to say, he starts to see God in everything. God says after you perform this ablution, that is, after you reach the station of annihilation, do whatever you do, because all ignorance or sin from your actions will be washed off. In a sense, there will be no ignorance in what you do. Everything you do will carry meaning and affect others. Your actions will not be sinful. This is the station of journeying with God, being with God in everything, in unity. It is being one with, or together with, God.

Q: When we cannot find water, "*teyemmum*," or dry ablution, is performed. What is the meaning of this?

A: *Teyemmum* is a means of purification. It replaces water when water is not available, since there is still a need for ablution. It is said that we can also use soil to cleanse ourselves, since, in addition to water, soil was one of the elements used in the creation of human beings. This also suggests that spiritual cleansing is possible first by opposing one's *nefis*, and second through continuous struggle. In other words, water is love, and the second part is struggling with the *nefis*. To be cleansed with water means to be cleansed with love. It is very easy. To be cleansed with soil means, "I don't have much love, but I do what you order with service and I'm trying to clean myself and get rid of all my bad habits." According to Rumi, this is like using a needle to dig a mountain. It is a truly tough and challenging task, but not impossible.

Q: Could you explain the meaning of the *tekbir* that is said during sacrifice, and the meaning of the *tekbir* that is said during prayer?

A: *Tekbir,* or the declaration "*Allahu Akbar* (God is Great)", is as if to say, "I have come to you as a sacrifice." What does this mean? "I seek intimacy and nearness with You. I rid myself of the excessive desires of my *nefis* in order to be near you and come to you in submission." This is the meaning of *Allahu Akbar*. "I do not exist; it is You who exists. In order to be intimate with you, I must accept your existence." God said to Moses, "Tell My servants that if it were possible, I would annihilate Myself for them, since two things cannot exist together. One must be annihilated in order for the non-existent to be united with the existent. My love for them is so great I would annihilate Myself for them, but I am the Eternal, Ever-living One Who has no beginning or end. So it is impossible for Me to annihilate Myself. Rather, they must become non-existent and come to Me in submission and humility."

Q: Through what stations does the *nefis* have to pass in order for it to be sacrificed?

A: The following stations are critical for the *nefis* to be sacrificed:

1. To be firm-footed on the path of *Şeriat*. What does it mean to be steadfast on this path? It means to obey all of God's commands. When a person falls in love, they happily do everything that their beloved wants, to the extent that they concede to the beloved's wishes and commands. If someone claims to be in love with God, wouldn't God want to see some evidence for this claim? Wouldn't He ask, "O My servant, why did you choose to obey your own (limited)

173

intellect? I taught you what you should and shouldn't do. But you used your reason to manipulate My divine commands. You presumed that out of My love for you, I would forgive you." In order for the *nefis* to be sacrificed for the Beloved, it has to first obey God's commands.

2. On the (Sufi) path it is critical to protect one's *edep*. What does it mean to protect one's *edep*? There is inner *edep* as well as outer *edep*. We must interact with others respectfully and with a smile. I was a teacher for twenty years, and each morning I would tell my students, "I urge you to start the day with a smile so that your day smiles back at you." I really believe this. Good conduct begins with good actions towards our own selves. This begins with a smile, which is among the few characteristics that distinguish us from animals. *Edep* constitutes good actions towards others because it stems from internal *edep*, which is to be able to see God in everyone and everything.

3. Also crucial is to remain connected to God during difficult times. This means to quit searching for reasons that caused the difficulty, but rather try and see the meaning of God in the difficulty. It is not important to pursue the cause, or to dwell on asking, "Why me? Why did such and such person mistreat me?" Mevlana Rumi says, "After every affliction, God manifests in your afflicted heart to console you on the condition that He finds you waiting for Him in the home of your heart. If you are not there and are instead seeking answers and explanations for your *nefis'* questions, then He does not find you, and you do not feel His consolation."

4. Finally, it is important to adorn yourself with divine attributes, to annihilate yourself in His attributes, and then to remember Him constantly. It is to feel the meaning of God with each breath that comes from *Hayy* (Everliving) and goes to *Hu* (He); to be given life with *Hayy*, through God's command, "Be!" and to return to *Hu* because of a life spent serving creation. Our teachers explain this state as one where "The hand is occupied in service and the heart is with the Beloved." It means for every human being who has attained this station, the wishes and desires of the *nefis* have been sacrificed.

Q: In sura *al-Hajj*, it is said, "It is neither their meat nor their blood that reaches God, but your piety. He has subjected them to you in this way so that you may glorify God for having guided you."[3] What does the meat and blood mentioned in this verse refer to?

A: The meat of the sacrificed animal represents the station of perfection (*kemal*). It tells us about this station of perfection, which enables a person to find the Perfected Human and to attain perfection. The blood represents the absence of the *nefis'* spiritual rights. This means that only nothingness and the adorning of ourselves with divinely sanctioned conduct takes us to God. It also tells us that we must sacrifice the wishes and desires of our *nefis* to reach the four stations mentioned above. Become a Perfected Human. It means when you perfect yourself, you become so beautiful that you are a source of betterment for those around you. This can be likened to the consumption of the meat that comes from you. The blood and meat in this verse indicate that you have reached a sublime station, thereby becoming a true and Perfected Human.

Q: In sura *Hajj*, God says, "to attain benefits and celebrate God's name, on specified days, over the livestock He has provided for them [for sacrifice] – feed yourselves and the poor and unfortunate"[4] What do the sacrificed animals in this verse refer to? What does it mean to feed the poor and those in need?

A: The sword or knife that slaughters the animal is the sword of opposition and the sword of effort. In other words, you cut and slaughter your *nefis* with the sword of the things or the people that create problems, harm you, or treat you poorly. Or you cut your *nefis* with the sword of effort that you exert in response to these problems and trials. So trial and affliction represent important swords that enable us to reach the perfect station. They allow us to cut the evil qualities that feed our *nefis*. Our own effort is equally important. There is a story in the *Mathnawi* on this topic, which I also mentioned earlier. Moses and Pharaoh entered a contest to see who could make the Nile flow upstream. They agreed that only the one who possessed God's meaning would be able to accomplish this feat. Moses was very relaxed. Confident that God was on his

---

3. Qur'an, *al-Hajj* (Pilgrimage), (22:37). Tr. Haleem, *Qur'an*, pp. 211-212.

4. Qur'an, *al-Hajj* (Pilgrimage), (22:28). Tr. Haleem, *Qur'an*, p. 211.

side and sure to help him, he slept soundly that night. Pharaoh, on the other hand, made immense effort; he prayed all night and pleaded with God, "O God! I know You exist. I believe in You. But because everybody else thinks of me and calls me 'god,' I can't do otherwise! Please, don't let this plea of mine go unanswered! I have been unable to conquer my *nefis*! Please don't let this effort of mine go in vain!"

The next morning, it was Pharaoh who managed to make the Nile flow upstream. Moses was shocked and asked God to help him understand. God said, "O Moses! You made no effort!"

So even at the station of prophethood, you are expected to strive and struggle. What is sacrificed, then, are the desires and wishes that stem from the *nefis*. These desires are slaughtered with the swords of trial, affliction, and effort. Slaughtering the desires takes a person to great heights. The path to God is then opened for that person. Once this path is opened, the person is made beautiful; they consume its meaning. And as they become more beautiful, they have an impact on their environment and on those around them; they exude inner peace and beauty. This is the deeper meaning of this verse; that they offer the same truth and its attainment to others.

Q: It is said, "Your sacrificial animals will be your beasts carrying you to paradise." What is meant by beasts here?

A: Beasts represent patience. The inner meaning of sacrifice is sacrificing the desires of the *nefis*, which carries the person to paradise. That which is developed through patience takes us to the true paradise of beauty. *Sabir*, the Patient, is also one of the beautiful names of God. But since it is the last of the ninety-nine names of God (according to a Prophetic *hadith*), it is the most difficult one to attain. Patience allows a person to reach Presence in the real sense. Let us not forget that the name of the gatekeeper of paradise is *Rıdwan*, or the most content. This tells us that contentment is the highest station and that the path to contentment passes through patience.

Q: Since we're on the topic of sacrifice, can we also talk about the historical episode of Abraham and Ishmael?

A: Abraham asked God for a child. God granted him this request, but with the condition of sacrifice. Abraham found that the love of

Ishmael had filled his heart. Yet, how could this love have entered Abraham's heart if God had not granted him Ishmael? Then came the divine command, "Sacrifice him, Abraham!" According to the actual story, that is what Abraham requested in reality. He had said in a supplication, "God, give me a child so I will sacrifice him for You." Similarly, "God, grant me manners that You dislike so I can sacrifice them for You!" It is the station of Adam, who took the apple and sacrificed himself for that apple. In pre-eternity, we pleaded with God, "Give us the wishes and desires of our *nefis*, O God, so we can fight against them!"

Q: Apparently we acted extremely ignorantly by accepting this trust. We were unaware of the burden it entailed.

A: Thank God that we were ignorant and from among those who loved to commit wrong, to oppress ourselves to such an extent that as a result we accepted God's trust. Of course, Mevlana Rumi says, "What else could Adam have done? The apple was love. Adam was love from head to toe. Love was driven to love." God said, "You are being sent down to earth, and you will suffer a lot. Don't say I didn't warn you. You will be extremely sad. You will be cast out of the heavens. You will face many trials." But Adam's hands were tied. He knew that trial and affliction would enable him to reach the highest station. So he sought affliction. Similarly, Abraham requested a child and was granted a child as a result of his request. Abraham's granting of the request is analogous to the human being coming to the world with his *nefis*.

This is similar to the saying by Mevlana Rumi: "Serpents guard the greatest treasures" or "There is no struggle unless there is an island." A place has to be captured for humans to then struggle for it. That is why Abraham was at a great station; he proved his rank magnificently; he submitted to his God. The day before Arafat[5] was when Abraham took all day reflecting on whether he was actually supposed to sacrifice his son. It is a very important day and must be spent in contemplation, where we must ask questions like, "Which parts of my *nefis* have I cut and which parts have I

---

5. Meaning the day during the Hajj pilgrimage on which Muslims travel to Mount Arafat from the city of Mina. Different components of the pilgrimage as performed today are symbolic reenactments of key events from Abraham's life, including the sacrifice of his son (reenacted at the culmination of the Hajj with the sacrifice of an animal).

failed to rid myself of?" Worship is very important on that day. It is a day on which we must be able to say, "I'm ready, my God, I am ready to give up that which is most beloved to me for Your sake!" There are some differences on the question of which son Abraham was told to sacrifice. 'Ali, Ibn 'Arabi, and other sacred personalities have said that it was Ishaq. But what is important here is that Abraham's son, either Ishaq or Ishmael, manifests through their saying, "Father, do as you are commanded."

There are two important points here. Abraham is at the station of the spirit. The spirit is ready to distance itself from the evil qualities of the *nefis*, but the *nefis* also has to be ready, so that the sacrifice of excessive desires is possible. Let's consider this event as it occurs in the body of a human being. There is a spirit, an intellect, a heart, and a *nefis*. If the *nefis* is not aware of the spirit's meaning or the meaning of God in the body, and if the light of the illuminated heart does not reach the intellect, the *nefis* is incapable and remains captive to its excessive desires. When the Light of God falls on the physical heart, it becomes an illuminated heart and the Prophet manifests.

All things that this light falls on are made visible, and this light directs itself towards the intellect. As it shines itself on the spirit, it tells the intellect, "Come on, see the spirit now." When the spirit is illuminated, the intellect begins to see it. The spirit then tells the *nefis*, "Know your nothingness. Where are you going, O traveler?" As soon as this question is asked, the *nefis* tells the spirit, "Yes, I'm ready. You are beautiful. I am the wrongdoer. I am a lover now. Come on, sacrifice all my excessive wishes and desires so I can be united with you." In this way, just like a sour grape, it demands to be transformed from its unripe state into a fully ripened state with the Light of God.

> Q: Is this similar to our teacher's saying, "Unless beauty (*cemal*) and majesty (*celal*) are united, no perfection (*kemal*) is possible?"

A: The manifestation of Majesty (*celali tecelli*) presumes an acceptance of the manifestation of Beauty (*cemali tecelli*). Majesty is God's essence and beauty is the acknowledgement of that essence. The Perfected Human, through his sacrifice, allows that disclosure to be known in himself. It is a station at which his *nefis* has transformed into *nefis* (*nefis* in Turkish also means wonderful), and this is what is meant by true identity (*hüviyet;* Ar. *huwiyya*) and by true character (*şahsiyet; Ar. shakhsiyya*).

Q: Thank you so much for joining our program; it has been such a pleasure.

A: I'd like to end with a couplet. We can summarize the meaning of prayer in two sentences:

> At times I exist and turn towards Your Beauty
> At times I cease to be and become Your Beauty

May God bless us with such a state.

CEMALNUR SARGUT

- *A Selection of Photos* -
Family
Teaching Venues
International Presence
In Turkey
Spiritual Affinities
The Media

During the recording of a TV show.

A post lecture discussion with audience in Istanbul.

182

Bottom row: Cemalnur with Esin Çelebi (from the twenty second lineal generation of Rumi's successors). Top row: Belde Aysel, Kerim Güç (Cemalnur's son), Dr. Asuman Sargut Kulaksiz (Cemalnur's sister), 2017.

With her students at an intimate gathering on her birthday in 2012.

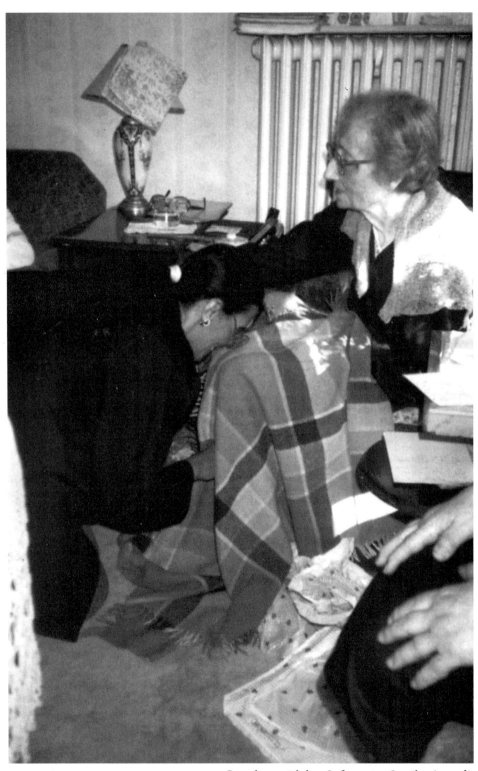

Cemalnur with her Sufi master, Samiha Ayverdi.

Kenan Rifaʿi, Cemalnur's spiritual teacher and prominent Sufi master of the Rifaʿi order.

At the launch of her book titled, *The Secret of Creation: Qur'an chapter 19, Mary, [verses 1-15]*, published by Nefes Press, in 2012.

Cover of Cemalnur's mother and teacher, Meşkûre Sargut's book, *From Heart to Heart*, published by Nefes Press in May 2014.

Class visit, UNC Chapel Hill, 2012.

Co-teaching Rumi's Mathnavi with her students at Altunizade Culture Center in Istanbul.

Small gathering for a lesson on Rumi's *Mathnavi*.

On Kenan Rifa'i's Anniversary, July 7th 2007.

Speaking as part of a series of lectures across cities in Anatolia, organized by the National Education Ministry.

Cooking with students.

Q&A after one of the weekly lectures on the *Mathnavi*, in 2011.

Cemalnur's students accompany her to Zimbabwe.

Cemalnur teaching a children's class in Dar al-Salaam, Tanzania.

On the occasion of the establishment of the Kenan Rifaʻi Chair at Peking University, China in 2011. Pictured with Dr. Tu Weiming, Dr. Sachiko Murata, and Dr. William Chittick.

Opening ceremony of the Kenan Rifaʻi Distinguished Professorship of Islamic Studies at Peking University.

Awarding of an honorary doctorate to Cemalnur Sargut by the Chancellor of the Eurasia International Research University, in Baku, Azerbaijan.

Press conference following the awarding of an honorary doctorate at the Eurasia International Research University. Pictured with Ganira Pashayeva (Member of Parliament).

Cemalnur Sargut and Naila Hayat at the Sufi Order International Conference, Lahore, Pakistan.

Cemalnur Sargut and Reza Shah-Kazemi at the Sufi Order International Conference, Lahore, Pakistan.

From left to right: Dr. Omid Safi, Dr. Juliane Hammer, Dr. Laury Maffly-Kipp, Cemalnur Sargut, Dr. Canguzel Zulfikar, and Dr. Carl W. Ernst at UNC-Chapel Hill in 2012.

Following a lecture in San Francisco titled "Living Sufism".

Cemalnur Sargut with Dr. Yasushi Tonaga in Kyoto, Japan.

After the signing of the agreement establishing the Kenan Rifaʻi Center for Sufi Studies at Kyoto University. From left to right: Emine Bağlı (Chair of Turkish Women's Cultural Association in Ankara), Cemalnur Sargut, Dr. Yasushi Kosugi, Dr. Yasushi Tonaga.

Cemalnur with Syed Salman Chishty (hereditary custodian of the Ajmer Sharif Dargah in India)

From left-to-right: Rahman Khan, Cemalnur Sargut, and Prof. Syed Liyaqat Hussain Moini at the Foundation of SAARC Writers Conference, Jaipur, India.

Speaking at the Foundation of SAARC Writers Conference, Jaipur, India.

Ajeet Cour, Arpana Caur and Cemalnur Sargut, at the Foundation of SAARC Writers Conference, Jaipur, India.

Commemoration ceremony for Gandhi's 60th death anniversary in New Delhi, India, 2008.

Gandhi's 60th death anniversary.

At conference titled "Intra-Civilizational Dialogue on 'Islamic Spirituality in the Contemporary World,'" in Kuala Lumpur, Malaysia, May 2005. With conference organizers, Dr. Azizan Baharuddin (seated) and Dr. Carl Ernst and Judith Ernst.

During Cemalnur's visit to Dhaka, Bangladesh for the International Science and Spirituality conference, 2008.

Visiting a Mevlevi Lodge in Bosnia, 2013.

During a visit to a Bosnian Women's NGO serving the female victims of the
Srebrenica massacre.

At the Haus am Dom, a Catholic conference & cultural center in Frankfurt, Germany.

At TÜRKKAD's Dost Award ceremony, pictured with Dr. Bruce Lawrence in 2012.

At TÜRKKAD Dost Award ceremony, pictured with Orhan Büyükaksoy (grandson of Kenan Rifai), 2012. The Dost Award ceremony is held annually on the Prophet's birthday to award one Turkish and one foreign scholar for their scholarly achievements and contribution to the study of Islam.

Opening of the exhibition of the Prophet's Cloak at the Topkapi Palace, Istanbul, 2008.

Sayyid family at the opening of the "One Servant One Messenger" exhibition at the Turkish Islamicate Arts Museum, Istanbul, 2007.

With Rifa'i Masters at the Harakani Symposium in Kars, Turkey in 2014.

At the Tasavvuf Institute, Uskudar University, with Dr. Nevzat Tarhan (Chancellor), Dr. Elif Erhan (Director of the Institute for Sufi Studies), and Ms. Hülya Deliktaş (secretary of the Institute).

Pictured with Selahaddin Çelebi Mawlana (from the twenty second lineal generation of Rumi's successors) and Dr. Asma Afsaruddin (recipient of the 2013 Dost award).

With Shaykha Nur Artıran of the Mevlevi Sufi order in Kars, Turkey.

Preparing for Kanalturk TV interview.

TRT 1 (Turkey's National Broadcasting Channel) show with Gülben Ergen.

Recording of Habertürk TV show with Oylum Talu.

Glossary

Ahadiyet; Arabic (Ar.) *ahadiyya*: absolute unicity [of God]

Ahlak; Ar. *akhlaq*: ethical conduct

akl-ı evvel; Ar. *al-aql al-awwal*: the first intellect

akl-ı kul; Ar. *al-aql al-kulli*: universal intellect

'arif / 'arif bi'Llah: gnostic/knower of God

aşk Ar. *ishq* Per. *eshq*: radical love

basmala: the formula "*Bismi'Llah al-rahman al-rahim* (In the Name of God, the most Beneficent, the most Merciful)" begins all but one of the 114 chapters of the Qur'an. The common Muslim practice of invoking this formula prior to any act – small or large – is a way to ask God to bless that act.

beşer; Ar. *bashar*: physically human

cemal; Ar. *jamal*: Divine Majesty; a divine attribute that carries the sense of God's overpowering force thus evoking a condition of awe in human beings

celal; Ar. *jalal*: Divine Beauty; a divine attribute that carries the sense of God's infinite mercy thus evoking a condition of intimacy in human beings

din: derived from the term dayn meaning debt, or the debt that humanity has towards God; din refers to thoughts, acts, and practices aimed at salvation. Often translated simply as "religion" though its varied valences encompass a range of meanings that go much beyond the modern concept of religion as reducible to scripture and propositional truth-claims.

edep: moral etiquette; or principles of conduct regarding God in every aspect of one's spiritual life

evliya; Ar. *awliya*: friends and lovers of God

Fatiha (Sura Fatiha): literally "the Opening"; title of the first chapter of the Qur'an; includes a total of seven verses which read as follows:

1. *Bismi'Llah al-rahman al-rahim*: In the Name of God, the most Beneficent, the most Merciful
2. *Alhamdu li-Llahi rabb al-'alamin*: All praise is for God, the Lord of the worlds
3. *al-Rahman al-Rahim*: the All-Merciful; the Compassionate
4. *Malik al-yawm al-din*: Master of the Day of Judgement
5. *Iyyaka na'badu wa iyyaka nasta'in*: It is You we worship; it is You we ask for help
6. *Ihdina al-sirat al-mustaqim*: Guide us to the Straight Path
7. *Sirat al-ladhina an'amta 'alayhim ghayr al-maghdubi 'alayhim wa la al-dalin*: the path of those You have blessed, those who incur no anger and who have not gone astray.

gönül: knowledge of the enlightened heart

hadith: literally, "report"; recorded sayings and actions of Muhammad

hadith qudsi: literally, "sacred report"; a narration or report that relates the words of God in the first person

hakikat: Divine Reality or Truth

hakikat-i Muhammadi; Ar. *al-haqiqa al-Muhammadiyya*: Muhammadan Truth

hakk Ar. *haqq*: the Truth; one of the ninety nine names of God; commonly used in Sufism to mean God.

halk Ar. *khalq*: the created; creation

Hajj: pilgrimage to Mecca, one of the five pillars of Islam

hamd: praise

hayy: the Everliving; one of the ninety-nine names of God

hu: literally, "he"; in Sufi literature, it signifies the essence of God and succinctly captures the idea of God as the singular source of all existence. It is used similarly in the Qur'an, as in the formula: "There is no god but He (*la ilaha illa hu*)" Qur'an 2:163.

hazret: literally "presence;" an epithet meaning one who maintains the state of being the presence of God.

hikmet; Ar. *hikma*: wisdom

hudur: peace (in Turkish usage); presence of heart and mind; in Sufism, the term carries the meaning of "spiritual presence" of a master.

hükm: law

hüviyet; Ar. *huwiyya*: essence; identity

'ilm: knowledge

iman: faith; one of the essential components of religion (*din*) along with submission (*islam*) and spiritual virtue (*ihsan*); in Sufism, the state of recognizing God in everybody and everything.

insan: human being

al-insan al-kamil: Perfected Human Being

'irfan: mystical knowledge

Ka'ba: cube-shaped structure in Mecca that holds pivotal significance in Muslim history and devotional life. According to the Muslim tradition, the Ka'ba was originally constructed by Abraham and Ishmael as a symbol of monotheism. However over time it became a central site for idol worship. After conquering Mecca in 630, Muhammad is said to have cleansed the Ka'ba of its idols and thus to have restored Abrahamic monotheism in Arabia. Muslims perform the five daily prayers towards the Ka'ba. Circumambulating around the Ka'ba is also a central ritual during the annual pilgrimage to Mecca (Hajj).

kader; Ar. *qadr*: destiny

kaza; Ar. *qada*: divine decree

kawthar: literally "abundance"; title of the 108th Qur'anic chapter, refers to the water of paradise, understood as a fount of divine grace.

kun: imperative command meaning "be!" *Kun* is stated in the Qur'an as God's creative-linguistic act that preceded the creation of the world. In the Qur'an, it also expresses the ease with which God can actualize the impossible.

kurban; Ar. *qurban*: sacrifice

al-lawh al-mahfuz (Preserved Tablet): the location of the Qur'an believed to be in God's presence; repository of all divine decrees; a term also associated with the eternal mother book (*'umm al-kitab*) that is the source of all heavenly scriptures including the Qur'an.

marifet; Ar. *ma'rifa*: spiritual knowledge

mihrab: prayer niche

mirac Ar. *mi'raj*: Muhammad's ascension to the highest Heaven

muhabbet; Ar. *mahabba*: compassionate love

murshid: spiritual guide

muslim: one who submits

nefis; Ar. *nafs*: ego-self

nur: light; one of the ninety-nine Names of God

rabb: Lord

rıza; Ar. *rida*: contentment

riyazat; Ar. *riyada*: continuous spiritual struggle

ruh: spirit

al-Samad: the Eternal; one of the ninety-nine Names of God

sayyid/sharif: a descendant of the Prophet

Şeriat Ar. *Shari'a*: literally, "path to water"; prescribed religious law intended to guide people to live and act in a way that aligns them with the Will of God; practically speaking, there is no single pre-existing Shari'a. Rather, it is an ideal or abstract norm that jurists strive to concretize through the process of jurisprudence which entails a consultation of the Qur'an, Prophetic Hadith as well as a range of other juridical sources and principles. In relation to Sufism, adherence to the Shari'a is the foundation or the first step on the Sufi path.

shirk: associating partners with God

sidre münteha; Ar. *sidrat al-muntaha*: literally, "lote tree of the farthest boundary;" is mentioned in the Qur'an, Sura Najm (The Star) (53:14). The first eighteen verses of this chapter are understood to describe the mystical ascension of Muhammad to the highest Heaven. They read as follows: "By the star when it sets! Your companion has not strayed; he is not deluded; he does not speak from his own desire. The Qur'an is nothing less than a revelation that is sent to him. It was taught to him by [an angel] with mighty powers and great strength, who stood on the highest horizon and then approached – coming down until he was two bow-lengths away or even closer – and revealed to God's servant what He revealed. [The Prophet's] own heart did not distort what he saw. Are you going to dispute with him what he saw with his own eyes? A second time he saw him: by the lote tree beyond which none may pass near the Garden of Restfulness, when the tree was covered in nameless [splendour]. His sight never wavered, nor was it too bold, and he saw some of the greatest signs of his Lord." (Tr. Abdel Haleem).

sohbet: spiritual discourse

şükür; Ar. *shukr*: thankfulness

sura: chapter in the Qur'an; there are 114

tekbir: the declaration "Allahu Akbar (God is Great)"

takva: God consciousness; piety

tarikat: Sufi Path

tasavvuf: Sufism

tecelli; Ar. *tajalli*: manifestation

tevekkül; Ar. *tawakkul*: having complete trust in God

teshbih: similarity [of God]

tevhid: oneness of God

vahdaniyet; Ar. *wahdaniyya*: the unicity of God

vahdet-i vücut; Ar. *wahdat al-wujud*: the oneness of being

veli Ar. *wali*: friend of God

vilayet:

zekat: alms

zikr; Ar. *dhikr*: remembrance [of God] session

PROPER NAMES

Ahmad: literally, "most worthy of praise"; epithet of the Prophet Muhammad

'Ali ibn Abi Talib (d. 40/661): often referred to as 'the Lion of God,' cousin and son-in-law of the Prophet Muhammad. Revered by all schools of thought, he is remembered as the fourth caliph in the Sunni tradition, and the first Imam (successor to the Prophet) in the Shi'i tradition. In Sufi literature he is often presented as the first Sufi saint.

Eid al-Fitr: festive celebration following the month of Ramadan

Eid al-Adha: celebration commemorating the end of Hajj and serves as a remembrance of Abraham's sacrifice of Ishmael.

Iblis: in the Qur'an, Iblis is the proper name for the devil, and the common name is *al-shaytan* or Satan. In her discussions, Cemalnur interprets Iblis and Satan as different stations or states of the human being: "Iblis is a more horrific station. Satan tries to lead you astray toward evil, whereas Iblis is what makes you say "I" and goads you into regarding yourself as better than everything else." (p. 21)

Idris/Enoch: a prophet, who is generally identified in the Muslim tradition with Enoch of the Bible. The Qur'an mentions his name twice, and says only that he was "lifted up to a sublime place." (Qur'an, 21:85-86)

Ilyas/Elijah: name given in the Qur'an to the Biblical Prophet Elijah (Qur'an, 6:85).

Khalil: friend; another name for the Prophet Abraham

Khidr: is a figure in the Qur'an who represents a quintessential spiritual guide and possessor of inner knowledge. Khidr is a highly revered figure in the Sufi tradition, the account of whose encounter with Moses (in the Qur'an, 18:65-82) forms a major literary narrative in Sufi intellectual thought and practice.

Mahmud: literally, "praised one"; epithet of the Prophet Muhammad

Mount Qaf: a cosmological mountain range marking the boundaries between the temporal and the heavenly realms.

Mount Arafat: also known as the mountain of mercy (*jabal al-rahma*), Arafat is a hill east of Mecca where the Prophet is said to have delivered his final sermon to the Muslim community. It is a central site during the performance of the annual pilgrimage (Hajj).

Mustafa: literally, "chosen one"; epithet of the Prophet Muhammad

Ridwan: literally, "the most exalted from among the contented ones"; name of the gatekeeper of paradise

'Umar ibn al-Khattab (d. 23/644): the second caliph according to the Sunni tradition

Zuleikha: Potiphar's wife in the Bible; her love for Joseph as recounted in the Qur'an serves as a powerful symbol of the helplessness of the lover (humans) before the Belovęd (God).

ARABIC PHRASES

Allahu Akbar: God is Great

Amantu bi'Llahi: I believe in God

Ashhadu an la ilaha illa'Llah: I bear witness that there is no god but
God

Bismi'Llah al-rahman al-rahim: In the Name of God, the most Beneficent, the most Merciful

Ana al-Haqq (Turkish *Ene 'l Hak*): I am the Truth

Insha'Llah: God willing

La ilaha illa'Llah: There is no god but God

La mawjuda illa'Llah: Except God nothing exists

La rahata fi'l-dunya: There is no ease in this world

Lam yalid wa lam yulad: He begot no one nor was He begotten

Rabbana laka'l-hamd: All praise is for You alone

Subhanaka: Glory be to you

Subhana Rabbiyu'l-'azim: Praise be to the Mightiest Lord

Subhana Rabbiyu'l-a'la: Praise be to the elevated Lord

Wa lam yakun lahu kufuwan ahad: No one is comparable to Him

Editor Biography

Tehseen Thaver is Assistant Professor of Religion at Bard College, USA. Her work centers on questions of Qur'an exegesis and religious identities in early and medieval Islam. She is also interested in the intersection of secularism, Sufism, and religious authority in contemporary Turkey. She is currently working on a book manuscript titled *Ambiguity, Hermeneutics, and the Formation of Religious Identity in Early Islam.* Her academic articles have appeared in the *Journal of Qur'anic Studies* and *Journal of the Royal Asiatic Society.* She received her PhD in Religious Studies from the University of North Carolina at Chapel Hill in 2014.